Fatal Friendship

By José Martí

Translated by Juan F. Zeledón

DEDICATION

To my dad Don Juan Francisco Zeledón,

To my mom Doña María Eugenia Tórrez,

To my daughter Isabella Rose,

To my family and friends!

CONTENTS

ACKNOWLEDGMENTS

I want to express my gratitude to the author, the critics and the readers of this novel!

CHAPTER ONE

The luxuriant shade of a great Magnolia, pruned by the house gardener, the one with the hands of an academic assistant, covered that Sunday morning the home family of Lucia Jerez. The huge white Magnolia flowers, fully open in its branches with large and shiny leaves, did not look like, under that clear sky in the yard of the lovely house, the flowers of a tree, but the flowers of the day. Those immense and immaculate flowers that one imagines when loves so much! The human soul has a great need of whiteness. Since white darkens, disgrace begins. The practice and consciousness of all virtues, the possession of the best qualities, the arrogance of the noblest sacrifices, are not enough to comfort the soul of a sole loss.

They were so beautiful to watch, that Sunday, in the fulgent sun, the blue light, and throughout the corridors with marble columns, the elegant Magnolia, among the green limbs, the big white flowers and the rocking chairs decorated with tape knots, those three friends on her May dresses: Adela, thin, talkative and attractive, with Jacqueminot's roses on the left side of her cream silk dress; Ana, about to die, hanging on her ill heart, in her white muslin dress, a blue flower tide up with a few streams of wheat; and Lucía, robust and deep, with no flowers on her filmy-silky crimson dress, "because the flower she loved the most, had never been seen in the gardens: the black flower!"

The friends switched vividly their Sunday impressions. Coming from mass; after smiling to their relatives and friends at the atrium of the cathedral, after walking around the clean streets, looking like smaltite of the sun, just like flowers laying on a silver plate with golden drawings. Their friends from the windows up in the big antique houses, had greeted them when passing by. Every single, elegant young man in the city was that noon around the corners on Victoria Street. The city, in that Sunday morning, looks like divorced. On the open doors from pair to pair, just like in that day no one would fear of enemies, the servants wait for their lords, clean dressing. The families, who just have seen each other during the week, gather right out of church to say hi to the blind mother, the sick sister, the ill father. The old men get younger that day. Veterans walking around looking up, so reluctant their white jackets, so neatly polished the cane knob. Employees look like magistrates. It is pleasant seeing artisans in their best velvet jacket, drill trousers well iron and his fine castor hat. Indians, really barefoot and filthy, among such clean place look like ulcers. The deluxe procession of fragrant mothers and fancy girls continues, planting smiles across the sidewalks of the animated street; and the poor Indians, who sometimes cross, look like caterpillars hanging of a garland. Instead of commerce wheelbarrows or merchandise drove looking, they fill the streets, pulled by brave horses, arrogant wagons. Even the wagons look content, just like victorious. The mere poor, look like the rich ones. There is a magnanimous tranquility and cast happiness. In the houses everything is huzza. Grandchildren going to the door and bothering the doorkeeper, impatient about what grandma is delaying! Grandmother, how loaded of groceries for her grandchildren, a whole lot of toys that accumulated during the week to brig them for the younger people, today on a Sunday, loaded of candy that just bought at the French confectionery shop, the whimsical eating mood of her daughter when she was younger, what a car grandma has, it never gets empty! At Lucía Jerez house no one would know rather if the Magnolia had more flowers, or there were more flowers in their souls.

On an open sewing workbox, where Ana after seeing her friends put among her sewing materials and the children furniture that she would give away to the Exposed House, Adela and Lucía had thrown her straw hats, with silk ribbons similar to their apparels, mixed like little fawns who are frisking. It says a lot, and very mischievous things, a hat that had been for one hour on a young lady's head! One can interrogate it, sure that will respond: from an elegant gentleman, and more than one, it is known that has stolen artfully a flower from a hat, or has kissed for a long time its ribbons, with a religious and charming kiss! Adela's hat was light and kind of odd, just like the one of a girl who is capable to fall in love of an opera tenor: Lucía´s was an arrogant and threatening hat: one could see the crimson ribbons on the edge of the sewing workbox, twisted on Adela´s hat like a boa on a turtle dove: from the bottom of a black silk, due the reflection of a sun light ray that was filtering between a Magnolia branch, it was looking like flames going out.

There were the three friends in that age where the characters are not defined yet: Oh!, In those markets where there is a tendency of the generous young men, who in search or blue birds, tide up his life to beautiful flesh cups that soon, with the first strong heats of life, show the astute fox, the poisonous snake, the cold and impassible cat who remains in the soul!

Ana´s rocking chair was motionless, just like in her pale lips the affable smile: the violet on her skirt had to be look for with the eyes. Adela was effortless on her rocking chair, sometimes was close to Ana, sometimes close to Lucía, and empty most of the times. Lucía´s rocking chair, more towards the front than laying back, would move suddenly in position, like showing obedience to an energetic and contented gesture of its owner.

-Juan is not coming: Am telling you, he´s not coming!

-Why, Lucía, if you know it so, you feel embarrassed?

-Don´t you think Pedro Real is so arrogant? Look, my Ana, tell me the secret you have to be loved by everybody: because that gentleman, must love me.

In a worked bronze watch, inlaid into a wide porcelain plate with blue branches, gave the two hours.

-See, Ana, see; Juan is not coming. -And Lucía did stand up; walked to one of the marble jugs between every two columns, there, from one side to the other did decorate the shady yard. She pulled of with no mercy from its shiny stalk a white camellia, and came back silently to her rocking chair, biting the leaves with her teeth.

-Juan always comes, Lucía.

In that moment through the golden grate that divided the antechamber entrance that open to the patio, a young man, dressed in black, who respectfully and tenderly was telling good bye to an older one, with kind eyes and a full beard, and an elder gentleman in his long years, sad, just like one who has lived so much, who was holding the young man hand with his:

-Juan, why you were born in this country?

-To honor it if I can, Don Miguel, as much as you have honored it.

The emotion was palpable in the face of the old man; he had not leave the entrance yet, holding the arm of the full beard one, when Lucía, her face quite altered and her tears shaking on her eye leads, she was standing up, straight with singular firmness, right next to the golden grate, and she said, staring on Juan her two imperious and black eyes:

-Juan, why you did not come before?

Adela was in that moment sticking on her blond hair a Cape Jessamine.

Ana was sewing a blue tie on a small newborn hat, for the Exposed House.

-I went to implore, Juan responded kindly smiling, to avoid pressing Mrs. Del Valle for the rent of this month.

-Sol mother? Sol del Valle?

And thinking of the poor widow's girl, who had not completed her school, where she was at the director's expense, Lucía went in, without looking back or looking down, through the bedrooms, meanwhile Juan, who loved the one who loved him, was following her sadly with his eyes.

Juan Jerez was a noble creature. Rich due to his parents, he lived with no selfish resignation that ruins the young man, neither with that anguish abundance, always lower than the expenses and appetites of his dreams, a matter that the rich who lack of common sense misspend on stupid employments called pleasures, their parents enterprises. By himself, and with his assiduous work, he had been attaining a great numerous reputation of a lawyer, whose mendacious profession, among others perniciously spread, they influenced him to start, more than his willingness, due to active and generous activities, his father's wishes, who in defense of honest cases of commerce had increased the properties contributing to the marriage with her wife. Therefore, Juan Jerez to whom nature had put that light cuirass that reinforce the friends of men, he came, because of those legendary preoccupations that violate and twist the life of new generations in our countries, passing by, between affairs of tribunal that sometimes made him feel anxieties and eversions, the most beautiful years of an impatient and mature youth, who would see in the inequalities of fortune, in the misery of the unhappy ones, in the sterile efforts of a vicious minority to create fecund and healthy towns, of solitudes as rich as lonely, of numerous populations of miserable Indians, an object more dignifying than the forensic efforts and heat of a noble and virile heart.

Juan Jerez was carrying on his pale face, the nostalgia of the action, the luminous disease of the great souls, decreased by the common duties or the random impositions to small tasks; and was carrying in his eyes like a desolation, that would change only when he would make the good, or when he worked on a worthy object, like a sunlight ray that enters into a tomb, in flashing joy. I would not be called a lawyer of these times, but one of those poets who knew how to measure up himself, tired already of his own songs, in the knob of his fiddle the hilt of a sword. The fervor of the knights did light in those brief instants of heroic fortune his good soul; and his pleasure, that would inundate him of a light similar to the stars, it was just comparable to the vast bitterness with he would recognize, at least the world cannot find assistance, but when a vicious interest is convenient, the purity works. He belonged to the selected race of those who do not work for success, but against of it. Never, in those small towns of ours where men get so crocked, neither in exchange of profits nor because of vaingloriousness Juan would cede an apex of what he believed sacred, that was his man judgement and his obligation not to put it with lightness or fee to the service of ideas or unfair people; but Juan would see his intelligence as a sacerdotal investiture, which has to be kept forever in a way that cannot be noticed by the parishioners; and Juan would feel himself, there in his determinations of a noble man, like a priest of all men, one by one he had to give them perpetual account, just like they were their owners, of the well use of their investiture.

And when he saw that, as among us happens frequently, a young man, of blazing word and privileged talent, he rented for the fee or the position of that divine insignia which Juan believed seeing in all superior intelligence, he turned the eyes on himself like flames burning him, as he would looking at the minister of a service, to pay for the drink or the game, would have sold the images of his goddess. These mercenary soldiers of the intelligence called him a hypocrite, which increased paleness of Juan Jerez, without taking of his lips a single complaint. Other said, with more appearance reason, -although not in his case, -that integrity of character was not largely deserved in whom, rich since little, did not have to sacrifice himself to open up his way, as our poor young men did it, in towns where old colonial traditions men are given a literary education, and yet this one incomplete and broken, does not find later on a natural employment in our unpopulated and rudimentary countries, exuberant, however, in live forces, nowadays misspent or barely worked, when to make prospered our lands and worthy our men, education is necessary in manner they can take advantage of their mother land so well provided where they were born. To manage the spoken and written language they teach them, as an only way of living, in towns where the delicate arts that are burn from the cultivation of the language do not acquire a large number, neither yet of consumers, even of people who appreciate who rewards, with the fair price of these exquisite works, the intellectual labor of our privileged spirits. In a way that, as cultivating intelligence come the expensive desires, so natural among Hispanoamerican people as the color of the cheek of a [fifteen years old girl; -as in the warm lands and flourished, wakes up early the love, which wants a house, and the best of cabinetwork to furnish it. And the most extremely glossy silk and the richest jewels to marvel everybody and make them suspicious in love to her owner; like the city, infertile in our new countries, keeps in its new-fangled webs those who out of it do not know how to earn the bread, neither those who cannot earn it in the city, in spite of their talents, as well as a wonderful sculptor of cup swords, who would know how to populate these ones of Castilians of long amazon passing out in the arms of strong warriors, and other subtle golden and silver beauties, does not find an employment in a small village of peasant people, who live in peace, or by the knife of the fists remit the terms of their disputes; as with our Hispanoamerican heads, loaded of European and North American ideas, we are in our own countries in a manner of fruits

[handwritten margin note: comparison to what a 15yr old girl is like]

with no market, like the excrescences of the earth, those that weight and are left, not as its natural flourish, it happens that those who posses the intelligence, sterile among us due its bad direction, and we need it to subsist and make it fecund, they dedicate it exclusive excess to the political combats, when nobler, producing therefore a misbalance between the narrow country and its bold politics, or, pressed by life urgencies, they serve the strong governor who pay and corrupt them, or they work just to overset him when, upset of new needy ones, he quit giving them the abundant salary for his fatal services. Out of these public troubles the one of the large beard was talking about, the elder man of the sad face, and Juan Jerez, when this one, connected since he was a child and in love to his cousin Lucía, he went into the entrance with marble polish tiles wide and white as her thoughts.

Kindness is the flower of the strength. The same vigorous Juan, who would always avoid fame occasions and parades, but barely visible, it was known about a privilege of the unknown motherland or because of the decorum and freedom of will of a humble man; that fearful and rough warrior, where no one took a chance to approach, embarrassed before hand, the offers and corrupting seductions where other vociferating people of venal temple had open their ears; that one who always had his pale face and dried like the splendor of a light high and unknown, in his eyes the flashing of a sword; that one who did not see the misfortune without believing it as a duty to be redeemed, and it was seen as a criminal every time he could not put remedy on a misfortune; that so lovely heart, whose over all abandonment was emptying his endless mercy, and over all humility, energy or beauty passionately wasted for his love, he had cede, in his life of abstractions and books, to the sweet necessity, so many times mournful, of pressing over his heart a small white knob. This one or the other one were not important for him; and him, in that woman, would see more the symbol of beauty rather than a real self.

What is running in the world under the name of good fortunes, and they are not, commonly, from one part or the other, more than hateful vilely, had left, one time and another, on the way of that young man whose face came, from the very inside of the soul, the irresistible beauty of a noble spirit. But those good fortunes, that in the first instant fill the heart of the overturning exhalations of the spring, and they give the men the worthy authority of whom posses an conquer; those occasional love affairs, honey in the edge, bile in the bottom, paid with the most valuable and expensive currency, the same of the mere cleanness; those irregular and frightened loves, elegant custom of low appetites, accepted due to vanity or unemployment, and gradually destroy life later on, as ulcers, only achieved in the courage of Juan Jerez to wake up the dread of, just an excuse or a charm name, live men an women, without falling death hating themselves, among such awkward imprudence. And he did not cede them, due the repulsion that inspired him, either his graces were, a woman whom next to her husband's work table or by her son's cradle did not hesitate to offer them, she was bigger than the painful satisfactions of complicity experienced in an honest man with an imprudent lover.

Juan Jerez had an unhappy soul that can only love the great and the pure. Genuine poet, who took out of spectacles seeing himself, of pains and surprises of his spirit, strange lines, deep and painful, looking like daggers pulled of his own chest, he suffered of the necessity of being beautiful as an ardent trickster, point out the selected of the songs. That serene reason, thinking that social problems or common passions did not ever darken, getting obscure until reaching prodigality of himself, in virtue of an excessive acknowledgment. There was in that character a strange and violent necessity of martyrdom, and in case the superiority of his soul was so difficult to find partners who animated and appreciated him, him, in need of giving himself, in his behalf wanted nothing, he saw himself as someone else´s property that he kept in his deposit, he gave himself as a slave to those who seem to love him and understand him with his delicacy or wish his wellbeing.

Lucía, as a flower that the sun crook over its weak stalk when its sparkling in its entire fire at noon; like every other overcoming nature needed to be overcame; in a confusing way and impatient, and with no order or humility that reveal la true strength, loved the extraordinary and powerful, and liked anxious horses, ascending up in the mountains, of tempest nights and of fat trunks; Lucía, who, still a girl, when she seem to get uneasy due the older people table talks, she forgot the games of her age, and taking the garden flowers, and watching the gold and silver fish swimming in pairs in the water, and combing the soft feathers of her last hat, to hear, sank in her chair, with her eyes open and shining, those wing words, large as eagles, those words that Juan always suppressed either in front of known or common people, but he would let plenty of them out of his lips, as javelins decorated with ribbons and flowers, it was barely felt, as a prosecuted bird in its warm nest, among good souls who listened to him with love; Lucía, in whom a wish would nail as hooks get stalked into fish, and having to resign to a wish, she remained broken and bleeding, just like the flesh when one takes off the hook from the fish; Lucía, with, her fleshy thought, had populated the sky she looked at, and the flower beds whose leaves she loved braking them off, and the walls of her house where she wrote with color pencils, and the pavement she used to largely watch while having her arms hanging over her rocking chair; out of that beloved name of Juan Jerez, wherever she looked there was a splendor, because she would fix it everywhere with her willingness and her look as the laborers in the fabric of Eibar, in Spain, they inlay the gold and silver threads on the black plate of emeried iron; when Lucía saw Juan entering, she felt sounds trembling in her chest some as harps with wings, and getting open into the air, as big as suns, some blue roses, straps in black, every time she saw him leaving, she gave him her cold hand with disdain, choleric for his leaving, she cannot talk to him, because her eyes got full of tears; Lucía, in whom the age flowers

obsessed with love

hide burning lava looking like veins of precious metals in the mines and felt like snakes in her chest; Lucía, who suffered for loving him, and loved him in an irrevocable way, and she was beautiful in the eyes of Juan Jerez, since she was pure, she felt one night, a night of her saint, where before leaving for the theatre she let it go to her thoughts with one hand on the marble mirror, that Juan Jerez, flattered by that magnificent sadness, would give her a kiss, long and soft, on her other hand. The entire bedroom seem to Lucía full of flowers; from the mirror crystal believed seeing flames coming out; closed her eyes, as are closed in all instants of supreme joy, as happiness had its modesty as well, and avoid her falling on the ground, those arms of Juan had delicately to function as a support to that body involved in white tulles, where in that hour of birth seem to bring out light. But that night Juan went sad to bed, and Lucía did it so, she stayed overnight by the window in her tulle dress, covered her shoulders in a blue air cloud, she felt, aromatized like a perfume glass, but serious and suspicious...

-My Ana, my Ana, here is Pedro Real. Look at him how arrogant!

-Get on your knees, Adela: get on your knees right now, responded sweetly Ana, turning to her the beautiful of curly and blond hair; meanwhile Juan, who came from making a peaceful agreement with Lucía refuged in the antechamber, she would walk towards the grate of the entrance to welcome the house friend.

Adela got on her knees, crossed, her arms on Ana's knees; and Ana pretended to cover her lips with a blue ribbon, and told on her ear, as someone who hold a shield or parapet of one move, these words:

-An honest girl do not makes public that she likes a wild, hot brained fellow, not until he had given her so many proofs of respect, so one could not doubt that he is soliciting her as his toy.

Adela got up laughing, and staring, among curious and scoffers, in the gentleman in full dress, who came holding Juan's arm towards them, she waited on them standing up by Ana's side, she with her serious mien, never tough, seem wanting to attenuate in favor of Ana herself, her excessive energy. Pedro, distracted and more friendly of butterflies than lovebirds, first greeted Adela.

Ana held for an instant in her thin hand Pedro's, and with those married lady rights who gives the young women the closeness to death.

-Here, she told him, Pedro: here this whole afternoon by my side.-Who knows if in front of that beautiful figure of young man, did not concern to the poor Ana, in spite of her priest soul, abandoning life! Who knows if she wanted only avoid that moveable Adela, overflying around that light of beauty, would hurt her wings!

Because that Ana was such, wherever she went, caused a splendor. And even when the sun sparkled, just as it was shining that afternoon, around Ana there was a clarity of a star. There were sweet creeks running for the hearts when in her presence. If she sang, with a voice that would spare deep inside the soul, as a light in the morning around the green fields, left in the spirit a gratifying uneasiness, as someone who has seem imperfectly, put for a moment out of the world, those musical clarities that only in the hours of making the good, or dealing with who does it, distinguish between his own fogs the soul. And that sweet Ana talked, would purify.

Pedro was good, and began to adore her, not the face, illuminated already by that light of death that attracts the superior souls and terrify the vulgar souls, but also the apparel of a child in which Ana was sewing the last ribbons. But she was not the only one sewing, and she fixed ribbons, and she tried them in different points of the hat for the newborn: suddenly Adela had turned into a great worker. She no longer jumped from a place to another, as she used to do it when talking a while ago with Ana and Lucía, but she had moved her chair right next to Ana´s. And she also, was going to be set next to Ana the whole afternoon. In her pale cheeks, there were two light dots that exceed in vividness to the hat ribbons, and heighten the impatient gaze of her eyes shining and daring. Her unquiet hair was getting loose, like wanting, free of nets, unfasten in free waves through the backbone. Due the nervous movements of her head, two or three leaves of the incarnated rose that would carry on her hair, felt on the ground. Pedro would see them falling. Adela, voluble and flippant, either with the little (sewing) basket, or messing up on Ana´s skirt the finery of the hat, or taking as useful the one she had just threw away giving a grimace of

FATAL FRIENDSHIP

impatience, or shaking and erecting for a moment the fine, rebel, and light head, just like the one of an untamed horse. On the white marble tiles would emphasize like drops of blood, the petals of roses.

Young people of our countries would talk about this trivial things during Sundays' reunions. The tenor, oh the tenor! had been admirable. She would die for the tenor voice. Francisco has an charming roll. But Mrs. Ramirez, how she had the braveness to dress in the colors of the party who killed her husband!, it is true she marries a colonel of the contrary party, who signed as an auditor in the process of Mr. Ramirez. The colonel is a good gentleman, a good gentleman. But Mrs. Ramirez has spent so much, she is not as rich as before; she had seven embroidering employees for a month to prepare the golden embroidery of the black velvet suit that brought to Rigoletto, it was very heavy. Oh! And Teresa Luz? so beautiful, Teresa Luz: well, the mouth, yes, the mouth is not perfect, the lips are too fine; ah, the eyes! well, the eyes are a little bit cold, they do not warm up, do not penetrate: but what a sweet inconstancy; they make one think of the spumes of the sea. And, how is going after Maria Vargas that little gentleman who came from Paris, with his verses copied from Francois Coppée, and his renting policy, what a wine, serving the opposition and he is a little less than the government! The father of Maria Vargas wants to be a minister, and he wants to be a deputy. He is so elegant. The hair is ridiculous, with the line in the middle of the head and the front head hidden under the waves. Not even for

17

women is good to cover the front head, where the light of the face is. The hair should make a small shadow with its natural waves; but why covering the front head, mirror where lovers see their own soul, white marble board where pure promises are signed, nest of the wounded hands in the desires of life? When one suffers so much, he does not wish a kiss in the lips, but on the front head. And the same small poet said it quite well the other day in one of his verses "To a dead girl", it was something like this: The roses of the soul rise up to the cheeks: the soul stars, to the front head. There is some of tenebrous and disturbing in these covered front head. No, Adela, no to Your highness it is charming the forest of little curls: that use to be the style of painting in old times the cupids fluttering over the front heads of the goddesses. No, Adela, do not pay attention: those covered front heads, scare me. One could thinks such things, that women cover their front head afraid to be seen. Oh, no, Ana: what shall you think of more than Jessamines and carnations? Oh well, no, Pedro: could you break the front heads, and you shall see inside, small pots that look like open mouths, some dry plants, that grow round and yellow flowers. And Ana was in this way making the conversation more noble, since God had given her the privilege of the flowers: the one of perfuming. Adela, had been quite for a moment, rose up the head and kept the eyes for while in front of herself, seeing how the Celtic profile of Pedro with his black beard, would emphasize with the sane light of the afternoon, over the marble socle that would put on one of the wide columns of the corridor in the house. She turned her head down, and within this movement, it did fall down the incarnated rose from her, falling into pieces to Pedro`s feet.

Juan and Lucia appeared on the corridor, she like regretful and submissive, he was like always, serene and kind. The couple was beautiful, just like the way the they were approaching to their group of friends in the backyard. Both of them were tall, Lucia, more than the normal one for her years and her sex, Juan, of that elevated height, aggrandized by the proportions of the forms, that has in itself some of a spirit, and looks prepared by nature to heroism and triumph. And there, in the penumbra of the corridor, like a ray of light on Juan`s face, and from his forearm, although a little behind, there was coming Lucia, on his front head, vast and white, it did look like a silver rose opening up: and from Lucia`s were seen just, in the dark shadow of her face, her two flaming eyes, like two menaces.

-Ana is impatient, Juan said with his charm voice: how come she has no fear of this crepuscular air?

-But this is my natural one already, dear Juan! Come on, Pedro: give your arm.

-But soon, Pedro, since this is the time when the aroma rise up from the flowers, if you don´t make her a prisoner, she would run away.

-This good Juan! It is not true, Juan, that Lucia is crazy? Adela and Pedro are on my side whispering, with appetite. Let´s go then, at this time fortunate people wish to have the chocolate.

The flagrant chocolate was waiting on them, served on an onyx table, in the pretty antechamber. That was a Sunday mood. The youth prefer always the disordered and the unexpected. In the dining room, with two old gentlemen, was arguing about the public matters Lucia`s and Ana`s uncle, a gentleman with silk hat and embroidery slippers. The grandma of the house, the mother of the lord uncle, would no longer go out of her bedroom, where she would remember and pray.

The antechamber was small and beautiful, just like it is necessary to be small to be pretty. Of braided crystal Tulips, suspended in a cluster from the ceiling by a hidden tube between Tulip leaves simulated in brass, was falling on the onyx table the orange and soft clarity of the lamp of incandescent electric light. There were no more seats than small rocking chairs from Vienna, of light lattice and black wood. The mosaic pavement of delicate colors that, like the one on Pompeian porticos, had the "Salve" inscription on the umbral, it was full of revolved benches, like those of a serving bedroom: since bedrooms must be kept pretty, not to shown them off, not for vanity, to visits, but to live in them. Improves and alleviate the constant contact with the beauty. Everything on Earth, in these black times, tends to affect the soul, all, books and paintings, business and affects, even in our blue countries! It is convenient having always in front of the eyes, surrounding, embellishing walls, animating the little corners where shadow finds a refuge, beautiful objects, that will color and dissipate it.

The antechamber was pretty, painted the ceiling with the Garlands boards of wild flowers, the walls covered, on their smooth frames of golden oaks, with paintings by Madrazo and Nittis, Fortuny and Pasini, imprints by Goupil; two by two were hanging the paintings, and every two groups, an Ebony little shelf, full of books, not wider than the paintings, neither taller nor smaller than the group. In the middle of the front porch that would face the door of the corridor, a slender column of black marble held an air tomb of Mignon by Goethe, on white marble, to whom feet, in a great glass of porcelain from Tokyo, with blue branches, Ana would put always Jessamine and Lilly pots. One time mischievous Adela had hanged on Mignon's neck a Garland of incarnated Carnations. In this fore self there were no books, neither paintings without imprints on life episodes of the sad little girl, and distributed like a halo on the wall surrounding the tomb. In the corners of the bedroom, on black trestle-horses, without black ornaments, would show off their rich binding four great volumes: "The Raven" by Edgar Poe, the fateful and heart-breaking Raven, with illustrations by Gustave Doré, that would take the mind to the vague spaces on the wings of horses without bridles: the "Rubaiyat" the Persian poem, the poem of the moderate wine and the fresh roses, with the apodictical drawings by American Elihu Vedder; a rich sample manuscript, clothbound on lilac silk, of "The Nights" by Alfred Musset; and "Wilhelm Meister" the book of Mignon, whose original past-board, overdone with insignificant arabesques, Juan had replaced, in Paris, for one of a black Morocco leather mate engraved with precious stones: topaz as clear as the little girl soul, turquoises, as blue as her eyes; not garlands, because there were not in that vaporous life; opals, like her dreams; a great and salient ruby, like her broken-swollen heart. In that particular gift to Lucia, Juan spent his earnings of a whole year. For the low areas of the wall, and like chairs, there were Ebony tripods, small Chinese glasses, with a lot of yellow but poor in red. The walls, painted in oil, with garlands of flowers, were white. That antechamber did cause, in which arrangement Juan influenced, an impression of light and faith.

And the five youths set down there, to taste in their cups the rich chocolate of the house, famous for doing it so fragrant. It was not that sweet, neither that condensed. For older people, the thick chocolate! Adela, capricious, asked for herself the most foamy cup.

-This one, Adela: Juan told her, putting in front of her, just before sitting down, one of the black coconut cups, in which the turnsole foam simmered.

-Damn it! Adela told him, while everybody laughed; you have given me the one of the squirrel!

They were cups, strange as well, which Juan, friend of motherland things, had known how the artificer combined art and novelty. The cups were of those little black coconuts of a perfect oval...those that the indigenous emboss with capricious labors and inscriptions, submissive these ones as their condition, and those pompous, bold and weird, so full of wings and serpents, tenacious memories of an original and unknown art that the conquest buried on the ground, by boats of lance. And these little black coconuts were so polished on the inside, and all over its exterior works in subtle relief as lace. Each cup rested on a silver tripod, formed by an attribute of some bird or wild beast of America, and the two handles were two precious miniatures, on silver as well, of the animal symbolized on the tripod. On three squirrel tails Adela's cup was resting, and the two squirrels were looking at her chocolate as seeing a sea of nuts. Two haughty quetzals, two quetzals with three feathers on their tails, the one in the middle long as green arrow, were holding the edges of Ana's cup: the noble quetzal, that when falls captive or sees broken the long feather of its tail, dies! The handles of Lucía's cup were two pumas elastics and ferocious, on the opposite side enemy fingers that waylay each other: were resting on three puma claws, the American lion. Two eagles were the handles of Juan's; and Pedro's, the one of good fellow Pedro, two capuchin monkeys.

Juan loved Pedro, as the strong spirits love the weak ones, and as, a color note or a grain of craziness, love, as such soft form of sin, the people who are not superficial to the ones who are.

Austere men have in the momentous companion of those crazy dandies the same pleasure genre that the family ladies who attend to a mask dance covering themselves with a vail that she may not be seen. There is certain spirit of independence in sin that makes it sympathetic when is not excessive. There are a few creatures on the world that, having themselves gums provided with tooth, decide not to bite, or recognize that there is a deeper pleasure than nailing the tooth, and it is not using them. Well, what tooth are for, the rest ask; even worse when they have them so good, but for showing it off, and triturate the tasty morse that they take to their mouth? And Pedro was one of those who just show off his tooth.

Unable, perhaps, of causing bad in conscience, the damage was such that he did not know when he caused bad, or, when satisfying a wish, he did not see any bad on it, but all of its beauties, for serious, it looked his, and on his own beauty, the fatal beauty of a lazy and ordinary man, he would look that as a natural tittle, lion tittle, on the goods of the land, and on the greatest among them, that are its beauty creatures. Pedro had in his eyes that troublesome flashing that subjugates and invites: in acts and words, the insolent firmness that brings the costume of victory, and on his same arrogance such forgetfulness that he had it, that was the greatest perfection and the most terrible charm of it.

Fortunate traveler; with the fortune of his mother short, for foreign lands, lost on them, where are little sins those that looks like infamies to us, that delicate concept about women, for great effort that the mind makes, without whose is not licit to enjoy, since it is not licit believing in love from the purest creature. All those pleasures that do not come rightly and on reason of legitimate affects, even if they were vanity Champaign, they are bitterness of the memory. That one with most honest, than with those who are not, for such time spending with squeezed fruits, the eyes become vicious in such a way that they do not feel more pleasure or art than squeezing fruits. Only Ana, among the young girls who he had met on his way back from the bad foreign lands, had inspired him, even before his illness, a respect that on his resting hours used to turn into a soft and persistent thought. But Ana would go to heaven: Ana who had never trust on that turbulent bachelor as the lord of her affable soul, as a nacre palace; but due that fatal perversion that attract the dissimilar spirits, he had not seen without a painful interest neither an exciting spring disturbance, that rich beauty of men, windy and firm, set it up by nature as vestiture to a poor soul, the same way some singers use to transport to affable swoons and ethereal spheres to his audience, with the expression on crystal and querulous notes, white as doves or acute as daggers, of passions where it coarse spirits are unable to understand neither of feeling. Who has not seen breaking of brutal acts and words against his delicate woman a tenor who had just sang, with over human power, the "Elegant Spirit" of the favorite one? such beauty over the poor souls.

And Juan, because of that security of the incorruptible temper, for that benignity of the superior spirits, for that inclination to the picturesque of the poetic imaginations, and because of boy ties, that do not fall apart without great pain of the heart, Juan loved Pedro.

They talked about the latest fashion, that green color has been rehabilitated, that in Paris, Pedro said, no more is lived.

-Well, I don´t, Ana said. When Lucía became a formal lady, where the three of us are going will be Italy and Spain: right, Juan?

-Right, Ana. Where nature is beautiful and art has been perfect. To Granada, where men achieved what has not been achieved anywhere on earth: to engrave on rocks his dreams; to Napoli, where the soul feels content, as it has come to its term. You will not want (to go), Lucía?

-I do not want you to see nothing, Juan. I will make in that bedroom the Alhambra, and in that patio Napoli; and I will build of mud-walls the doors, and so we will travel!

Everybody laughed; but Adela had started walking to Paris, who knows with what partner, the happy wishes. She wanted to know it all, not about that tranquil and given internal life, on the stove heat, reading the good books, after discretely taking a glance among the French novelties, and studying with great ardor as much artistic richness as Paris involves; but the theatrical and nervous life, the museum life that is generally lived in Paris, always standing, always tired, always painful; the life of theater heroines, of the people who show off, ladies who become crazy, of the nabobs who captivate everybody with the bountiful employment of their fortune.

And while Juan, generous, giving loose to the impatient spirit, was taking out of Lucía's eyes, so she would getting her temper quite, and he was getting prepared for the existence travel, the luminescent inners of his peculiar and elevated soul, and he would say things that, because of the nobility that they would teach or the happiness that they promised, they force to become visible tears of tenderness and mercy on the eyes of Ana, Adela and

Pedro, in fullness of France, came and went, as holding hands on the forests and boulevards. "Judic no longer wears Worth. The hands of Judic is the most beautiful of Paris. In racings is where people are sporting the best clothing. How pretty Adela would be, on a racing coach-box, on a very soft yellowish Tilia dress, ornamented with silver passementerie! Oh, and with a guide like Pedro, who was so familiar with the city, how soon she would be knowledgeable of everything! Over there one does not live with all these troubles of around here, where all is bad! Woman is here a disguised slave: over there she is the ruler. That is Paris now: the kingdom of women. Here, everything is a sin: if she goes out, if she goes in, if she holds hands with a friend, if she reads a pleasant book. But that is a lack of respect that is acting against works of nature! Just because a flower germinates in a Sevres glass, it should be lacking of air and light? Just because women is born prettier than men, her thought should be oppressed, and using the excuse of a hypocrite honor, obligating her to live hiding her impressions, like a thief hides his treasure in a cave? It is precise, Adelita, it is precise. The prettiest women of Paris are the South Americans. Oh, there would not be in Paris other so sparkling like her!"

-Look, Pedro, interrupted at this point Ana, with that smile hers that made more efficient her displeasures, let Adela stay quite. Do you know that I paint, right?

-She paints little pictures that seem like music; all of them full of a risen light; with a lot angels and seraphim. Why don´t you

27

show us the latest, my Ana? It is beautiful, Pedro, and extremely marvelous.

-Adela, Adela!

-It is really marvelous. Is like a corner of a garden and the cycle is clear, so clear and so pretty. A young man... such a nice fellow...dressed on such an elegant gray suit, he looks at his hands astonished. He has just broke a lily, that has fall to his feet, and his hands have been stained with blood.

-What do you think, Pedro, about my painting?

-A positive success. I met a painter from Mexico in Paris, Manuel Ocaranza, who made things like those.

-Among gentlemen who break down or stain lilies I would love my painting to be successful. Who would actually paint, and not having those mistakes of mine! Pedro, mistaking or not, as soon as I get better, am going to make a copy for your honor.

-For me! Juan, is it not this the time in which seeing a gentleman kissing hands to the ladies was well seen?

-For your honor, but under the condition that you will hang it on a place so visible for yourself. And why we are talking about masterpieces right now? Oh, because your honor talked to my Adela about Paris. I will start another painting as soon as I get better! On a hill I will paint a sitting monster. I will put the moon on zenith, so it will fall fully on the monster´s back, and allows me to simulate with lines of light on the salient parts the most famous buildings of Paris. And while the moon charms him the back, and it seems by contrast of the luminescent profile the whole blackness of his body, the monster, with woman head, will be devouring roses. Over there by a corner young skinny and disheveled girls will be seen escaping, with their broken tunics, raising their hands to the sky.

-Lucía, Juan said badly holding his tears, to the ear of his cousin, always amazed: what if this poor Ana dies!

Pedro did not find opportune words, but that confusion and uneasiness that the people given into superficiality and joy experience in the intimate company of one of those creatures that pass by the earth, in a vision way, placidly getting extinct, with the happy capacity of foretelling the pure things, superhuman, and the beauty indignation for the battle of furious appetites where it is consumed, the earth.

-About monsters, I know two types, Ana said once: one dresses on skins, devours animals, and walk on claws; the other one dresses on elegant suits, eats animals and souls and walks with an umbrella or a stick. We are nothing but reformed monsters.

That Ana when she was in intimacy, used to say these singular things. Where has the poor girl suffered so much, just out of the circle of her venturous house, where she had learned to know and to forgive? One lives before living? Or stars, willing to take a recreational trip to earth, for some time tend to find themselves a place on human body? Ay! That is why the bodies with stars last so short.

-So, Ana paints, and "The Arts Magazine" is seeking paintings by authors from the country they portrait, and this sinner Juan has not made publishing those wonders on "The Magazine"?

-This Ana of ours, Pedro, gets annoyed as trying to bring her to light. She does not want her paintings to be seen until she judges them quite perfect to resist criticism. But the truth is, Ana, that Pedro Real is right.

-Pedro Real, right? Ana said with a crystal laugh, of a generous mother. No, Juan. It is truth that the art things which are not absolutely necessary, must not be made when one can make them perfectly right, and these things I make, that I see alive and clear deep in my mind, and with such a reality as am feeling them, they turn later on canvas so counterfeited and hard that I believe my visions will punish me, and they reprehend me, and take my pencils from the box, and myself of an ear, and they take me in front of the painting so I will see how hotheaded they delete the bad painting I made out of them. And then, what shall I know, with no more drawing than the one Mr. Mazuchellí taught to me, with no more colors than these pale ones that I take out of myself?

Lucía followed with unquiet eyes the physiognomy of Juan, deeply interested in what, one of those moments of explanation of themselves who enjoy having who feel something inside and feel like dying, Ana was telling. What Juan that one, who had her by his side, and was thinking of something else! Ana, yes, Ana was so good; but what a right Juan had forgetting about Lucía, and being by her side, paying so much attention on the weirdness of Ana?

When she was by his side, she must be his only thought. And compressing her lips; turned into high color, as an eversion of blood her cheeks; she was nervously wrapping with the pointing finger of her left hand a quite fine handkerchief of batiste and thread lace. And she wrapped it so much, and she would unwrapped it up with such violence, that going from one hand to the other, the pretty handkerchief looked like a viper, one of those white vipers that one sees on the Yucatan Coast.

-But that is not the reason why I do not show my paintings to someone, Ana continued; because while am painting them, I either get so happy or so sad like a dement, without knowing why: I jump for being content, even when I cannot jump that much, when I believe I have given by a touch of pencil to a pair of eyes, or to the widow lovebird that painted last month, the expression I wanted; and if I painted a misfortune, it seems to me it is real, and I spend hours looking at them, or I get upset of myself if turns into those I can not remediate, as in these two little canvas of mine that you know, Juan, "The Mother without Son" and the man who dies on a chair, looking on the chimney the extinct fire: "The Man without Love". Do not laugh, Pedro, of this collection of extravagances. Neither assume that these issues are for older people; the ill ones are like little old ladies, and have the right to this boldness.

-But, how? Pedro said subjugated, how come your painting do not have all the enchainment and the opal color of your soul?

-Oh! Oh! Adulation: realize it is not of good temper being a flatterer. Adulation on the conversation, Pedro, is as Arcadia on painting: a matter of beginners!

-But, why did you say, Juan said here, that you did not exhibit your paintings?

-Because since I imagine them until I complete them I go putting on them so much of my soul, at the end they do not become canvas, but part of my same soul, and I get embarrassed if one saw it, and it looks to me I have sin by daring such issues that are better as clouds than colors, and since I am the only one knowing how many doves holds, and how much violet it opens, and how many stars illuminate what I paint; only I feel how my heart hurts, either my whole chest gets full of tears or my temples are beating, as if the wings would be whipping on them, when am painting; since nobody else knows that those pieces of canvas, even when they turn so unfortunate, they are pieces of my inner soul where I have put the best of my will the best in myself, it feels like a pride thinking that if I show them in public, one of those wise critics or presumptuous intriguers would tell me, for sporting a recent name just learned of a foreign painter, or a pretty phrase, that this thing I do is by Chaplin or by Lefevre, or my little painting "Living Flowers", where I have discharged on it a shotgun full of colors! Do you remember? As if I did not know that a person I have not met, as I had not studied two or three people of a same temper, before symbolizing the character of a flower; as if I did not know who is that red rose, proud, with black shadows, that rises up over the rest of them on its stalk without leafs, and that other blue flower that is looking at the sky as it were turning into a bird and tending its wings, and that pretty Christmas box that prudently hikes, like a punished boy, over the stalk of the red rose. Bad ones! Shotgun charged of colors!

-Ana: I will surely take you, with your root, like a flower, and in that great Indian glass that is on my writing table, I will have you eternally, so my soul would never get disconsolate.

-Juan, Lucía said, as holding and getting up: do you want to come and listen to "M´odi tu" that you brought Saturday? You have not listened it yet!

-Ah! and by the way, don´t you know, Pedro said as he was getting up to say good bye, that the ideal head that has published in his latest number "The Arts Magazine"...

-What head? asked Lucía, one who looks like a virgin by Raphael, but with American eyes, with a figure that seems like the calyx of a lily?

-That one, Lucía: since is not an ideal head, but the one of a girl who will leave the coming week out of school, and say that is an amazement of beauty: it is Leonor del Valle´s head.

Lucía got up with a movement that looked like a jump; and Juan grabbed from the ground to return it to her, the handkerchief, broken.

CHAPTER TWO

About twenty years before the story we are telling, came to the city where it happened, a gentleman of middle age and his wife, both born in Spain, from where, in strength of certain untamed condition of the honest Don Manuel del Valle, who was badly seen by the people in power as a leader head and speaker of the liberal ideas, decided at the end to leave Sir D. Manuel; not necessarily because was insufficient the sustenance his gentle lawyer office of a province, but because always had, to stay or to move, to the small cherry, as they called over there to the police, on top of him; And because, consequently of wanting pure liberty and for good purposes, he remained with a few friends among those who look like defending it, and they would see him as an offensive warden, and this helped him to determine, of a hit on the head, coming to "the Republics of America", imagining, that where there was not superficial queen, there would not be oppressed people, neither that crowd of courtesans and lazy flatterers, who look like terminated shame of his race to D. Manuel, and, for being a man, as an own sin.

It was a never ending thing, and having to implore him to calm down, when with that picturesque language and unembarrassed he remembered, with his well intolerance of thunder and lightening and great threats as towers, the sly works of so and so marchioness, who helping someone else´s superficialities wanted to do, commonly, least guilty their own; or such story of a captain of wardens, that looked good in court with his rude beauty of a highlander, and his abundant and messy hair, and as soon as he realized of his good fortune he borrowed some money, to curl his hair with the stylist, and in terms of the tailor dressing of a good woven stuff, and good boots, so he would look elegant by the time of the visit to palace, when the Captain came back with these gracefulness, seemed on the other hand so ugly and presumptuous that was very close to loos more than captaincy. And of some tours, and parties in the country, talked in such a way D. Manuel, as well as about certain dinners at the fond of a Frenchman, who while telling about them he cannot be sitting; and he would hit the nearest table with his fist, as accentuating words, and thunders would get lauder, and he would open at his reach many windows or doors. The good all Spanish gentleman became disfigured, of holy ire, which, like embarrassed after giving reins on land that was not his, would always end up D. Manuel playing the guitar he had brought during the voyage, with such a tenderness that used to moisten his eyes and everybody else´s, some serenades of his own music, other than the Aragon's fable that worked as a beginning and a kind of short ritual, had a desperate love song of a dead troubadour of them for the lady of a hard Castilian, in a castle, over there behind the seas, where the troubadour would never see.

In those days the pretty D. Andrea, whose long braids of grey hair were the envy of many who knew her, she was exact in some cooking abilities, she brought from Spain, foretelling that would please her husband later on. And when in the book room, that was actually the living room, was sparkling D. Manuel, shaking instead of putting on shoulders alternatively the edges of the cover which arguing of being cold, would rarely take off, it was fixed that he was getting in and out of the kitchen, with his elegant and modest body, the good all lady D. Andrea, putting hands on a Mancha pisto, or dressing some fritters of Salamanca that she had asked her relatives in Spain, or preparing, with more willingness than art, rice with ham, of which exquisiteness, that had just calmed the ire of the republican, never say bad thing D. Manuel del Valle, even when deep in his mind he would recognize that something was burned there, or suffered major accident: or the ham, or the rice, or both. Out of motherland, if one received black stones from her, from black stones seem to rise up light as of off stars!

Was made of fine steel D. Manuel, and so honest, that never, for so many hurries he had, dedicated his intelligence and knowledge, neither excessive nor poor ones, to the service of so many powerful and intriguers who are all over the world, who would make end of an agony to those needy people, as long as theses would help with their abilities the success of the ways in where they promote and support their fortune: in a way that, if one looks at it, people are living today with so many tricks, it is even of bad taste being honest.

In this and that daily life, the country did not step well, wrote Mr. Valle with expert hand, even though a little febrile and ruined, his drubbings against the monarchies and the vileness it generates, and its hymns, in high tone as battlefield songs, in praise of freedom, where " the new fields and the high mountains and the wide rivers of this beautiful America, look like natural sustenance".

But shortly to this, twenty five years had passed to the date of our story such things have been seen by our lord D. Manuel who took the cover again, which for useless he had hanged on a corner of the closet, and each day he was getting calmer, and writing less, and rolling himself better in the cover, until he kept the feathers, and used to the clement temperature of the country and to the sweet treatment of his sons to consider in abandon it, he determined opening a school; even when he did become expert in the art of teaching, since this art was not well known in Spain either, such novelty that would accommodate better the Hispanoamerican easy and ardent, than the fool methods in use, in that way with his Iturzaeta and his Arithmetic by Krüger and his Lineal Drawing, and some prominent lessons of History, were Felipe Second was escaping and laughing as devoured in flames, the lord Valle graduated a generation of disciples, a bit of romantics and given into the wonderful, but they were to their time gentlemen of honor and tenacious enemies of tyrant governments. In such a way, for matters like putting Felipe Second in his place, the lord D. Manuel was about going, with his cover and his notebook by Iturzaeta, to hit on the hands of the American small cherries "in these very Republics of America". At the date of our story, about twenty-five years had passed.

The lord D. Manuel was such a housekeeper that even before the disciples celebrate the first anniversary, with a chicken, with a pair of doves, with a turkey, the presence of a new ornament in the house.

-And what has been, D. Manuel? Any Aristides who had to free the motherland from the tyrant?

-Be quite your honor, country fellow: quite your honor: one more Malakoff! (Malakoff, they were called this way back then, due the famous tower in the war of Crimea, what has been called just Miriñaque or Crinolina)

Lord D. Manuel loved his sons so much, and he promised himself living long time for them; but there was a little pain on the left side of his chest some time ago that was truly bothering him, as a small basket of flames that would be there lit, days and nights. And would never turn off. As when the little basket would burn him with more strength he felt a bit paralyzed the arm of the heart, and the whole vibrant body as the cords of a violin, and after this would come abruptly feeling of crying and a necessity of lying on the ground, that would make him so sad, that good old D. Manuel did not see without joy as soon as more sons were coming to life, that in case of his death would have to be more of an obstacle than a help for "that poor Andrea, who is a woman, such a lady and kind, but; for a bit, a bit!"

Five daughters had D. Manuel del Valle, although before them a son had been born, who

start showing signals to be the soul of a worthy man. He had weird preferences and extreme braveness, no so much to deal with his friends, even though he did not run away to deal with them in case it was necessary, as to confront difficult situations that required something more than the strength of the blood or the nimbleness of his fists. Once, with a few fellows of his, published at school a mini-handwritten newspaper, and of course a revolutionary one, against certain pedant teacher who prohibited to his students to argue about the things he taught them; and as an aficionado of the pen he would draw as a turkey to this teacher, on a page delivered with the mini-handwritten newspaper, and D. Manuel due the complain of the turkey, threaten in the same principal room by expelling out school through a code of conduct to the author of such a discourtesy, even if it was his own son, gentle Manuelillo, proud primogeniture of the eminent gentleman, he wanted to take off his fellows all fault, and take it entirely over himself; and getting up from his chair, said, with great perplexity about the poor D. Manuel, and muttering of admiration of the assembly:

-Well, Mr. Director: I did it alone.

And he would spend the nights in clear, after the poor candle would extinguished itself, reading with the light of the moon. Or he would go out for a walk, with the "Empresas" by Saavedra Fajardo under his arm, on the shady streets of the Alameda, and believing sometimes he was an incarnation of great figures of History, which germs he would feel in himself, and others feeling desperate for doing the things that could make him equal to them, he would start crying, of desperation and kindness. Or he would go at night to the seashore, to feel on his face the fresh drops that jumped from the salt water when crashing on the rocks.

He read as many books as he got in hand. He would ride as many horses as he had to his reach: even better if he found it unsaddled; and if they had to jump a fence, even better. In one night he would memorize the books his fellows did not in a whole academic year; and even the Natural History or Universal History and whatever add something to his knowledge and stimulate the judgement and verb, they were his favorite matters, with just a few turns of pages penetrate the sense of the most obscure Algebra, so much that his master, an engineer well known and rude, offered to teach him, in award of his dedication, the way of calculate the infinitesimal.

Manuelillo would write, similar to what it was in fashion by then, letters and articles of customs that would reflect already a young lover of fine language; but quite soon he started flying with hi own force, and began to correct the presidents who do not direct honestly to their people, some odes so much like Pindaric ones, and so well received among the students, that in a revolt against the government some Patricios who were so lonely and carry with them a good doctrine, was captured Sr. Manuelillo, who really had a seditious microbe in his blood; and so the reach friends of D. Manuel had to step up really well to free the Pindarito due the grace of his age, to whom his father, scolding him with the lips, where his mustache was shaking, as trees when the rain is going to fall, a approving him with the heart, send him to take, in what he made big mistake, studies of Law at the University of Salamanca, a disfavored on compared to others in Spain, and not so glorious now, but the place where miserable Mrs. Andrea had the good relatives who send her the fritters.

The one of the odes left in a brigantine that had come loaded of wines from Cádiz; and set on the poop of the ship, he would fix on the coast of his motherland the eyes so full of such a sad manner, that in spite of the new eagle that he carried in his soul, he thought he was all dead and with no capacity to resurrect and he felt he was like a tree planted in that coast for its roots, to which the vessel was carrying offshore from its branches, in a way that the tree remained rootless, if the force of the vessel had taken it off, and died: or as the trunk could not resist that pulling off, it would get broken at the end, and died too: but what Manuelillo would clearly see, was that he died anyway. Which, oh! Was true, four years later, when from Salamanca had found that boy the way to spend, as a tutor in the house of a Carlist aristocrat, going to study in Madrid. He died of enemies fevers, starting with big headaches, and painful visions and tenacious that he described in his revolved bed, of delirious, with nonsense and furious words, that felt like a box of broken jewelry; and indeed a vision always in front of his eyes and he thought it would come on top of him, and would vomit a fire like air on his front head, and left with bad humor, and came back to him from far away, calling him with many arms: the vision of a palm tree on a flat land. In his land, the flatness that surround the city were cover by palm trees.

D. Manuel did not die due the mourning of his son´s death, even thought he could feel it; but two years earlier, and without Manuelillo knowing it, he set one day on his chair, so cover by his cape, and with the guitar by his side, as he felt in his soul some very sweet music, at the same time as a freshness humid and flavorous, that was not the one of everyday, but even greater. Mrs. Andrea was set on a stool to her feet, and, saw him with her eyes dried, and grown, and had his hands. Two daughters cried in a corner: the oldest one, more valiant, charmed him with the hand his hair, or entertained him with flatterer phrases, while preparing him a drink; suddenly, by getting away Mrs. Andrea´s hands rapidly, D. Manuel opened the arms and his lips as looking for air; he closed them violently surrounding Mrs. Andrea´s head, to whom he kissed in the front head with a frenetic kiss; he got upright as he wanted to stand up, with the arms to the sky; he felt on the leaning-stock of the chair, so his body crashed horrendously, as when the furious thunder a wild vessel moves the chain that holds it to the seaport; his face was filled with blood, as in his interior the glass that keep and distribute it had been broken; and white, and smiling, with his hand casually hanging over the hand of his guitar, he died. But Mrs. Andrea never wanted to tell it to Manuelillo, to whom people tell him his father did not write him due arthritis on his hands, so he would not fear and perish in the house, and would want to save them, interrupting before time his studies. And it was also that Mrs. Andrea knew her poor son had been born full of those wills of redemption and evangelical Quixotery that had made sick the heart of his father, and accelerate his death, and since the land they lived in there was so much to redeem, and so many captive things to free, and so many crooked to make straight, the good mother would see with extreme fear, the hour when her son come back to his motherland, which time, to her point of view, would the one of Manuelillo´s sacrifice.

-Ay! Mrs. Andrea said, one time a friend of the family talked to her full of hopes about her son future. He will be unhappy, and he will make us even more unhappy without loving him. He loves so much others, and so little to himself. He does not how to make victims, but he knows how be a victim. Fortunately, even in anyway, for deceitful of Mrs. Andrea, Manuelillo had departed from the land before seeing his own, behind the burning palm tree!

Who is the one that seeing a broken glass or a building in ruins, or a palm tree fallen, does not think of widows? Strengths were not enough for Sr. Manuel, and, in foreign land this had been too much, barely to cover decorously with the products of his work the domestic needs. Even to help Manuelillo staying in Spain, had put him in great difficulties.

These times of ours are insane, and with the fall of the great social barriers and the fitness of education, a new vast class of aristocrats of intelligentsia had been created, with all the needs of showing off, and with the rich wishes that come from it, without being a time even for, during the rapidness of the event, for the switch of organization and distributing of fortunes would correspond to the tough alteration of social affairs, produced for the political freedom and the vulgarization of knowledge. A neat enterprise is the extract of universal happiness. Therefore, look for in the people, in the houses, in the most secure love itself, the reason of so many disorders and failures, that darken it and make it ugly, when they are not a cause of a division, or death, which is another form of it: the enterprise is the stomach of happiness. Husbands, lovers, people who still have to live and you wish to prosper: organize very well your will!

From this unbalance, almost universal today, suffered the house of Sr. Manuel, obligated with his media of a poor man to provide for themselves, even though with no waste of money, as a rich gentleman. Who would regret, if they love them so well, their beloved sons, brilliant and intelligent learn these things of art, drawing, painting, playing the piano that make a house so happy, and elevate, if they are well comprehended and fall in fertile soil, the character of whom possess them, those things of art that barely a century ago were almost an exclusive property of queen and princesses? Who sees their little and delicate ones, in spite of that aristocracy of the spirit that in these new times have substitute the degenerate aristocracy of the blood, does not want to dress them on such a pretty way, according to his own cultivated desire, who does not get enough with falsifications and banalities, and in a way that dressing will complete and reveal distinction of the soul of the beloved children? One, big father now, with the heart pumping and the wrinkled front head, content himself with a black suit well polished and spotless, which, and a decent face, one is well set and well received everywhere; but, for women, to whom we had made suffer so much! for sons, who make us nuts and ambitious, and put us, in the heart of insanity of wine, and in our hand the weapons of the conquerors! For them, oh, for them, everything look so little!

In such a way that, when Sr. Manuel died, in the house there were only the things of his use and ornament, where one would guess the good knowledge of freedom, the books of Sr. Manuel, that the mother saw as living thoughts of her husband, that should be kept neat for her absent son, and the things of school, that a helper of Sr. Manuel, who took most of his disciples when he saw Sr. Manuel dead, he found the way to buy the widow, abandoned by the one consciousness of that who must continue supporting her, in a short term, although the greatest seen after Sr. Manuel death in that poor house. The palm trees make one think of the fallen widows.

This or that friend, is true, wanted to know every now and then how well the poor woman was doing. Oh! They were so luckily interested in. She knew already: when she required so, all she need was to order it. For anything, for everything they were her servants. So, they came in a solemn visit, in a feast day, when it supposed to be people at the house; and they left doing so many courtesies, as with the ceremony of them, they wanted to make forget the greatest intimacy that could obligate them to provide a more active service. It is scary seeing how lonely the house remains where disgrace had entered: one wishes to die.

What Mrs. Andrea would do, with so many daughters, two of them so well grown; with the son in Spain, even though the young noble had prohibited, even assuming his father was alive, the transfer of money? What would happen to her little daughters, who were, the three, for modest and united, the glory of school; with Leonor, the last flower of her entrails, that one stopped by people down the street just to look at their pleasure, admiring her beauty? Where should be Mrs. Andrea? There, the trunk cut, the branches of the tree get dried, once green, and abandoned over the land. But never the books of Sr. Manuel! Those ones were never touched: no more than for cleaning them, in the little space set in the house, such a poor house that she took right there, the lady allowed to enter once a month. Or when, certain Sundays, the rest of the girls went to the house of a friend to spend the afternoon, Mrs. Adrea would enter alone the bedroom, holding Leonor's hand, and in the shadow of those books, set on the chair where her husband died, she would fly away on mental conversations, that seems to make her so well, since she left them in such a stage of silent majesty, and as cleared of her face and erected in high; in a way that the daughters when came back from their visit, always knew, for the major softness of her moves, and the expression of painful happiness of her face, if Mrs. Andrea had been in the room of books. Leonor was never looking fatigued going with her mom in those interviews: but, even when she was ten years old by then, she set on her mother laps, close to her breast or hugging her neck, or she would lie by her feet, leaning on her knees her head, with fine hair the widow played, distracted. Occasionally, a few times, she would grab her in a rapid move in her arms, and kissing with tender craziness the head of the girl she would start a quite bitter cry. Leonor, silently, would wet the hand of her mother with her kisses.

From Spain, Sr. Manuel brought a few things, and Mrs. Andrea even less, who was of a poor and noble. All of them, little by little, to attend the needs of the house, was leaving her: even some Margarita pearls an uncle had brought from America to Salamanca, grandfather of Mrs. Andrea, and an emerald avocado from the same origin, that she received from her parents as a wedding gift; even some silver spoons and glasses that were brand new when the mother of Sr. Manuel got married, and this one would show to his American friends, to prove in his hours when he did not trust freedom, how more solid were the times, things and artifacts of old times.

And all the wanders of the house were falling in hands of
indecent buyers; an autograph scene from "The Honest
Delinquent" by Jovellanos; a collection of Roman and Arabic
coins from Zaragoza, from which Arabic stimulated fantasy and
would make Manuelillo´s eyes brighter every time the father let
him be curious on them; a letter from Mrs. Juan the Crazy, who
never was crazy, unless not loving well is not craziness, in such
letter, written with the hands of secretary Passamonte, such worth
things are said and so tender that would make those who read it, to
fall in love of the queen, and sweetly touched in their entrails.

In this way two other jewels Sr. Manuel had appreciated so
much, and shown to his friends with the fruition of a fond guy who
gets pleasure by giving them a dish which recipe is decided not to
let them know ever: a wooden study of the head of San Francisco,
by Alonso Cano, and a drawing by Goya, with red pencil, sweet as
a head by the mere Rafael.

With the silver spoons a month of the house was paid: the
emerald was enough for three months: with the coins they helped
themselves for half a year. An impudent bought the head, in a day
of anguish, for fives pesos. A little bit they helped themselves that,
very bad collected and so scolded, earned Mrs. Andrea and the
older daughters to some small girls from the poor neighborhood
where they went to find a shelter from their pains. But the drawing
by Goya, that was actually, well sold. That one, by itself, produced
as much as the margaritas and the silver spoons, and the avocado.
The drawing by Goya, the unique jewel that Mrs. Andrea did not

regret to sell, since it brought a friend to her, it was bought by Juan Jerez; Juan Jerez who knowing that Manuelillo had died in Madrid, and the mother consummate by the expenditures due a serious illness of her girl Leonor, realized one day thinking with consternation it was necessary to sell them all, he bought the books to Mrs. Andrea, but he did not take them with him, leaving them to her instead "because he did not have a place to put them, and when he needed them, he would ask them to her". The world has to be such a mean one, and Mrs. Andrea already knew that the world is usually mean, so she satisfied her impulse and kissed Juan's hand.

But Juan, young rich and from parents and friends who did not assume Juan should look for a wife in that humble and helpless house, understood that he should not visit it, where they were already happiness of his eyes and heart, more for their honesty than their beauty, the two older girls, and so distracted the thought in things of the highest, and so fine and generous, and so tied for the acknowledgment of love that was been shown to his cousin Lucia, neither he frequently visited the house of Mrs. Andrea, nor he boasted of not visiting her, as he brought her his own medical doctor when Leonor's illness, and came back when the sell of the books, and when he knew some affliction of the lady, that he could with his influence, not with his money that used to become poor, it can have a remedy.

What, as a night lily in a dark room, had in the middle of all these agony illuminating the soul of Mrs. Andrea, and made sure in his noble believes in human being novelty, was that, he felt sorry for the luck of the widow, he believe one had to seem bad, being like beloved Sr. Manuel, and master as her, so they would let the daughters out of school due the lack of payments, the principal of the Institute of La Merced, the most famous and rich one of the country, made one day, in a beautiful wagon, a visit, that was well known, to the house of Mrs. Andrea, and while there she told her magnanimously, such a thing that right away she vociferated and celebrated so much the press, so the three girls would received in their school, if she did not send it anyway, all their education, as external, without such cost. Yes, that time Mrs. Andrea, without the considerations that in case of Juan had to avoid it later on, covered with kisses the hand of the principal, who treated her with a beautiful-pontifical excellence, and as an immaculate woman treat a guilty one, after which she came back to school so pompous, in her arrogant wagon.

The girls did not really tell Mrs. Andrea that, even though there were no other such dedicated as their, neither those with such white and iron little dresses, nor, in class or break would show better behavior, the notes of pardon given by the teachers during the weekends, and the first positions in tournaments, and the awards in exams, were ever for them; the scolds, yes. When the girl of the minister had spilled the inkwell, surely it was the minister's girl, how come the daughter of the minister? It was one of the three girls del Valle. The daughter of Mr. Floripond, the powerful baker, the ugly one, the big bones, the messy, the full of envy Iselda, had hide, where could not be found, her box of pencils to draw: of course, the box did not appear: "All the girls had money to buy their boxes! The only ones who did not have money over there were the three del Valle!" and they were checked, the poor ones, who allowed them to be checked with the face full of tears, and the arms in a cross, when by fortune the girl of another banker, not as rich as Mr. Floripond, said that she had seen Iselda putting the box of pencils in Leonor's bag. They were so good, and kind, so close they set to each other the three of them, with or without playing with themselves, during the break; with such gentleness they obeyed the most unfair and inharmonious mandates; with such a submissiveness, for the love of their mother, they stand those rigors, where the helpers of the school, lonely and helpless they themselves, started treating them with some tenderness, commend them to the copy of the class list, to sharp their pencils, to distinguish them with those little favors of the teachers who put the children so calm, and the three daughters or del Valle would compensate with great pressure in serve them and a modesty and such grace, that would gain the hardest souls. This kind disposition from the helpers rouse to the point when the principal, who did not have sons, and was still a very pretty woman, gave signals to become aficionado of Leonor, who some afternoons would let her eating in her table, sending her later to Mrs. Andrea with an affectionate message; and a Sunday took her for a tour in her wagon, showing herself visibly thankful than day responding with her best smile to all the greetings.

Because those who posses a good condition, if they procure it implacably in others when due the position or age of these ones feel fearful to become rivals, they please themselves, in contrast, for a type of prolonged egoism and for a strength of attraction that seems unique and of a divine nature, in recognizing and proclaiming in others the condition they posses, when it does not become an obstacle.

They love and admire each other in which, out of this danger of rivalry, have the same conditions of them. They see them as a renewal of themselves, as a relief of their faculties that decay, as if they had seen themselves as those new creatures, and not like they are becoming. and they attract them to themselves and they hold them to their side, as if they wanted to fix, so it will not escape, the condition they are feeling is already abandoning them. There is, additionally, great motive of pride in hearing to celebrate the type of merit from one distinguish himself.

True is that there was not a better way to call the attention on taking Leonor closely. What a look, that seemed a pledge! What an oval of her face, the most perfect and pure! What a skin, it did look like giving light! What a charm in all herself, and what a harmony! At night Mrs. Andrea, as being the youngest of her daughters she had her always in her bedroom, she did not see her well while asleep, she uncovered her to see her better; she moved the hair of her front head and she put it behind to see her neck, she took her hands, as grabbing two doves, and she carefully kissed them to her; she fondled her feet, and covered them with slow kisses.

A carpet would love to be Mrs. Andrea, so her daughter would never hurt her feet, and so she would walk on her. Carpet, a ribbon for her neck, water, air, all she touched and needed to live, as if there were no other daughters, she wanted to be for her Mrs. Andrea. Leonor used to wake up when her mother was contemplating her in this way; and not quite opening her loving eyes and attracting toward herself with her arms, she felt asleep again, with the head of mother between them; of her mother who almost slept.

How the poor woman suffered when the principal of the school, when Leonor was thirteen years old, came to see her, as someone bringing a great service, and in reality it was for Leonor future, so she would remain at school as an intern student! In the first instant, Mrs. Andrea did feel like falling on the ground, and, wordless, she stared the principal, as an enemy. Only by thinking of it, she felt as someone had pulled her heart off her breast.

She murmured thanking. The principal understood she accepted.

-Leonor, Mrs. Andrea, is by her destiny due her beauty to call the attention in such an extraordinary way. She is a girl still, and now you see your Honor how the fame of her beauty is all over the city. Your Honor will understand how difficult is to me having her as an intern student at school; but I believe is my obligation, for the care to your Honor and the lord Sr. Manuel, completing my work.

And the mother seemed as wanting to put ahead an objection; and the beautiful woman, who in reality, in the strength of the placid beauty of Leonor, had conceived for her a tender affection, she said promptly these good reasons, that the mother saw shinning in front of herself, as burning knives.

-Because your Honor, Mrs. Andrea, that Leonor position in the world, will be extremely delicate. The situation you are reduce into force all of you to live apart from society, and in a sphere in which, due the mere natural distinction and due the education she is receiving, she cannot find a proportionate husband for herself. Completing her education in my school as an intern student, she will interact more, during these three years, with girls more elegant and rich from the city, who will become her intimate friends; I will go myself taking care specially to favor those friendships that can be more convenient even more when she gets out to the world, and will help her to keep herself in a sphere where in no other way, with no more than her beauty, in the position where you are, she will never achieve. Pretty and intelligent as she is, and moving in good circles, it will be easier for her to inspire the respect of young fellows who in a different way would chase her without respecting her, and find by chance among them the spouse who make her venturous. It does scare me, Mrs. Andrea, said the principal who observed the effect of her words in the mother, scares me to think of the luck Leonor will face, as beautiful as she will be, in the helplessness where you have to face, even worse if you happen to be absent for her! You think about it your Honor that we do need to protect her of her own beauty.

The principal, now with mercy of the great pain reflected in the factions of Mrs. Andrea, who did not show strengths to open her lips, wishful to reach with adulation her eagerness, she had taken the hands of Mrs. Andrea, and she hugged them kindly to her.

Leonor entered in this instant, and in the point of seeing her, it was as the torrent of cries tied by the agony would jump out at the edge of her eyes; she said no words, but unforgettable sobs; and she run into the encounter of her daughter, and she hugged with her extremely close to her.

-I will not go, mother, I will not go: Leonor told her to her ear, so the principal did not hear; although Leonor had told to this one that, if Mrs. Andrea wanted so, she wanted to go.

To the few moments Mrs. Andrea, pale, set next to Leonor, to whom she was holding her hand, could finally talk. Because it meant to let it go of what was left from Sr. Manuel, to those loved nights of hers in silence, in which her soul, lonely with her bitterness and with her girl, remembered and lived; because the further he would get, in her daughters, and in Leonor, as a symbol of all, had become refigured, with the clearness of simple souls who have strength only to love; because giving Leonor was as giving all the lights and all the roses in life!

She could finally talk, and with a voice opaque and low, as someone talking from far away, she said:

-Well, well, lady. God will pay you for your good intention. Leonor will stay at school. We had already seen at the beginning of the story that Leonor was about to get out of it.

CHAPTER THREE

What would be the topic of the conversation of the whole city, but gossiping about Sol del Valle? It was as the morning that follows the day when a powerful orator had been revealed. It was like the dawn of a new drama. It was that inevitable revolt that, even its ingenious vulgarity, men experience when suddenly appears in front of them a supreme quality. Later, they get together, in silence first, then openly, and they talk about what they admired. They turn upset of getting caught. They turn so deafly angry, for seeing in others the condition they do not posses. And, the more intelligence they have to understand its importance, the more they hate it, and so they hate the unhappy one who posses it. At the beginning, pretending they are not envy, they act like they accepting it: and, is of strong not fearing, they put an extreme courage to adore the same one they envy, but little by little, and without saying a thing to each other, united by the common anger, they are forming groups, gossiping, telling revelations to one another. They have been exaggerated. Well seen, it is not what they said. The same thing has been seen before. Those eyes must not be hers. Surely she delineate her lips on crimson. The line of her spine is not so pure. No, it is not so pure. It looks like there is a wart on the back. It is not a wart, but a wen. It is not a wen, is a hump. People end up having a hump in their eyes, in such a way that they really see it on the back of a person, because has it on oneself! Ea! That is for sure: men who never forgive those who they have been obligated to admire.

There, in a corner of the chest, sleeps like a drowsy doorkeeper the need of greatness. It is fame that for adding champagne its fragrance, they distill each bottle, for unknown procedure, three drops of a mysterious liquor. The need of greatness, as these three exquisite drops, is in the bottom of the soul. Sleeps as it ever will be awake, oh, it tends to sleeps so much! Oh, there are souls where the doorkeeper never wake up! Has a deep sleep, in things of greatness, and even worse in these times, the human soul! Thousands of little goblins, or repugnant figures, spider hands, swollen belly, light mouth, double lines of teeth, rounded and lustful eyes, constantly turn around the sleeping doorkeeper, and they add in his ears poppy juice, and they put it near by him so he can breath it, and they put it on his temples, and with very delicate pencils they wet the back of his hands, they set on his laps, they set on the back of the couch, looking hostilely everywhere, so nobody will get close and try to awake the doorkeeper: How greatness tends sleep in the human soul! When gets awake, and open its arms, at the first move sends the little goblins with swollen bellies running away. Then the soul put an effort on being noble, ashamed for not being for such a long time. It is just that the little goblins are hidden in the backs of the doors, and when hungry tease them again, since they have promise to eat the doorkeeper little by little, they start letting the poppy aroma going out, which in a way of thick furbelows goes disturbing the eyes and watching the front head of the defeated doorkeeper; is has not been too long since he set the goblins away, when they come already back into confusion, they climb down the windows, they let themselves falling for the sides of the doors, they go out of the broken blocks of the floor, opening their big mouths in a lough that does not sound, they climb so agilely by his laps and arms, and one of them step on his shoulder, the other sets on his arm, and all of them agitate up high, with a noise of a gnawing rat, the poppy. Such is the sleep of the human soul.

What could be the conversation of the whole city, but Sol del Valle?

About her, because they about last night party: about her, because the party unexpectedly reached, due the influence of that girl who was unknown yesterday, an elevation and enthusiasm that not even the same who contributed to it will ever reach again. As stars tend to gather in the sky, ay! Just to hit and destroy themselves almost all the time, there, with no a better destiny, they tend to reencounter on earth, as they did last night, the genius, and that other genius, the beauty.

* * * * *

Preceded with special fame the Hungarian pianist Keleffy had come to the city. Born rich, and enriched even more because of his art, he did not travel, as others, in search of fortune. He traveled because he was full of eagles, that ate his body, and wanted wide space, and they got drown in the city jail. He traveled because he married a woman who he believe loving her, and he found later on as a deaf cup, where the harmonies of his soul did not find echo, he become so sorrowed that the poor athlete-musician had no strength, he could barely move his hands to play the piano: until a loyal friend took him from the arm, and told him "Get cure", and took him to a forest, and the to the sea, whose music entered into the half dead soul, they remain in it, seating and with their heads up, as lions who are scenting the desert, and finally they went out to the world again in such sudden fantasies where Keleffy was extemporizing while on the boat for the seas, those fantasies were such, that if one closed the eyes when hearing them, looked like rising up in the air, getting bigger when higher, so radiant stars, on a sky of a deep and fearful blackness, and other times, as in the light colorful clouds one was drawing a wreath of wild flowers, of a so pure blue, from where baskets of light were hanging: What music is, but the guide and partner of the spirit on its trip for the spaces? Those with eyes in the soul, have seen what would make Keleffy extemporizing his fantasies on the sea: there are others, who do not see, they refuse so showy what they have not seen, others would see. Surely a mole have ever been able to conceive an eagle.

Keleffy traveled across America, he has been told that in our sky of the South the stars look like anywhere else, and he heard of some flowers of ours, huge as the head of a woman and white as milk, that grow in the countries of the Atlantic, and about some wide leaves that grow in our exuberant coast, and take off mother land and lay voluptuously on Her, as the arms of a deity dressed on Garlands, that called, permanently open, those who do not fear of loving mysteries nor goddesses.

That pain of living without love, and with no right to inspire it nor accept it, since he was attached to a woman whom he did not love; that pain did not sleep, neither have peace, neither wanted to leave his chest, and had trapped his fantasies as snakes, that would give to his whole music an air of combat and torture that he tend to save it from balance and harmonious proportion so artwork need that; that pain, in a beautiful spirit who, in the species of loving pest is cheating the world in the old towns, had saved, as a wounded dove, a close feeling to the chaste one; that pain, that sometimes with the crisped hands the poor musician would look for into his heart, as taking it off from the root, even if he had to take his heart with himself; that pain would not let him a point of restless, it would make him look extravagant and shy, and even though the softness of his look and the ardor of his speech he would get the attention since the first time, as one who subdue, the willingness of those who saw him, little by little he would feel how in those affects the deaf hostility was getting in as the common spirits persecute men of superior souls, and that type of fear, but horror, when men, hungry of pleasures, run away, as from a stinky, of whom, under the grief of misery, neither knows how to give happiness, nor has the will to share them.

* * * * *

Now in the city of our story, whose rich people had all gone, in more than one chance, on a trip to Europe, even in those houses without pianos, and, what is even better, no one who would play it with such natural good styles, Keleffy had numerous and ardent friends; among the big-brains, for the exquisite art of his compositions, as well on the young and sensitive people, due the melodious sadness of his romances. When everyone knew Keleffy was coming, not as an artist in exhibition but as a man who suffers, the elegant society determined to receive him with the most beautiful celebration, they wanted to be the biggest one the city had ever seen, because of Keleffy ′s talent people would say marvelous things, because this good old city of our story did not want to be less than others in America, where the pianist had been greatly fondled.

In the "marble house" they decided to celebrate the big party: with a red carpet covered the wide steps; the corners, the living rooms, the patios, were full of palm trees; in every single rest of the main steps there was an enormous Chinese glass full of Camellia flowers; a pretty living room, the one of receiving, was hanged of yellow silk; from Fig trees hidden by the curtains a noise of fountains aroused. When someone entered the room, at that fresh spring night, with all the balconies open to the night, with so many beautiful women dressed on light clothes of soft colors, with so many feather fans, so fashion then, moving with pauses, and with that vague tremor of a party that just starts, it looked like entering an enormous wing basket. The top of the piano, up to bring more sonority to he notes, appeared, as dominate them all, a huge black wing.

Keleffy, who discerned the sum of real affection mixed in that celebration of curiosity and felt since his arrival to America as there were on constantly in his soul two big black eyes; Keleffy for whom was sweet not finding a house, where his last pains, thrown into his romances and nocturnes, did not find tender or friendly hands, that would bring them to his ears like tuned and on the way to consolation, because "in Europe one plays-Keleffy said-, but here one charms the piano"; Keleffy, who did not notice disagreement between the chaste way he loved his magnificent art, and that generous and discreet party, where one could feel the attendance as permeated by respect, on the moving and pleasant sphere of the extraordinary; Keleffy, in such mournful and melancholic manner, and more of who is going away than the one who is arriving, he played the black wooden piano, the one looking like a psaltery under his hands, sometimes a flute, sometimes an organ, some of his delicate compositions, never those where he sang telling the sea climbed the mountains and felt broken into crystals, or a man fighting with a bull and he would split its nape, and he would bend its legs, and put it down to the ground, but those flexible fantasies where, having color, they would have been pales, and being visible things, they would have looked like a crepuscular landscape.

* * * * *

Then, a sudden tremor was heard in the room, similar to those during the national celebrations at the crowd´s at the plazas when a clung of stars breaks in the air the artifice fire. It was well known that there was a beautiful girl at the Institute of La Merced! that girl was Sol del Valle; but no one knew she was so beautiful! And she came to the piano; since she was the lovely disciple of the Institute and no one like her understood that pledge by Keleffy, "Oh, my mother!", and he played it, tremble at the beginning, later forgotten in his music and therefore prettier; and when he got up from the piano, the tremor was one of astonishment in front of the beauty of the girl, not because of the talent of the pianist, not common somewhere else; and Keleffy saw here, as she were taking part of him with herself; and, while seeing the way she walked, the audience gave a big applause, as music had never stop, as feeling pleased by the visit of a deity of superior spheres, or proud of being a human being, while such a beauty one was among humans.

How she was? Who knew it better than Keleffy! He saw her, saw her with desperate and miserable eyes. She was like a cup of nacre, where nobody has yet put his lips on. She had the beauty of the dawn, the dawn that enchant and ennoble. She was like a palm of light. Keleffy did not talk to her, but he looked at her. The girl, when she set by the side of the principal, almost break into tears. The revelation, the first feeling of one´s own power, pleases and scares. The girl feared , even though she does not answer yes, delighted by that rumor as her front head was touched with very soft feathers, she felt lonely and at risk, and she looked for with her eyes, on an anguishing glance to Doña Andrea. Oh! Doña Andrea whom, the older she was, she was sinking into herself, just to see better don Manuel, in such a way that was already, if she always smiled, she barely talked. She talked so quickly. All the eyes were on her. Who is she? Who is she? Women do not celebrate her, they straighten up on their chairs to see her; they moved their fans so fast, they gossiped to its shade with a partner; they would turn to see her again. Men, felt in themselves as a broken rein; and others as a broken wing. They talked with unusual animation. They gathered in circles. They measured her with the eyes. They envisioned holding her hands showing in the room, tightening her by her waist during the ardent and daring dance; they meditated the echo mystical phrase, for which they should impress while being introduced to her. "So, that is Sol del Valle?". "What houses she visit?". "I am a friend of the principal, come on!". "Who will introduce her to us?". "Poor girl!" She never saw her bedroom as those curious men would figure it out. A sacred piece is not for most men, nor a cup of spirit beauty; but a tempting apple. If there was a lens that would allow women to see, as they see how thoughts move around men craniums, as well as the things they hold in their hearts, they would love them so much less.

It was not a man, no, the one who looked at her with more insistence, with a certain rancor mixed with loved, looked to Sol del Valle, with difficulty hold his tears that would come close as waves to his eyes, open, where his eye lids could barely move. Knew her in that moment, and already hated and loved her. Loved her as a sister. What mysteries of these brave and furious natures! Hated her with an irresistible and tragic dislike. When a courteous and handsome gentleman, who saluted much people on his way, approached her, since he lived in the highest social sphere, more than saluting her, to protect Sol del Valle, when Juan Jerez came at the end by the side of the girl, and Lucia Jerez, who was the one looking at her, saw them together, closed her eyes, recline her head on her shoulder as one who is dying; her face turned all yellow; and only at the end of a moment, to the concurrence of the air that her friends agitated with their fans, she open her eyes again, they looked opaque, as a black eagle had crossed on her thoughts.

Keleffy in those instants had the audience subjugated and voiceless. There her pure hopes of other times; his agonies of a sad husband; the disorder of a mind that escapes: the sea is later peaceful; flora is all American, rich and ardent; the shady shortening of the unhappy soul in front of the beautiful nature; one as an invasion of light that had flashed the atmosphere, and had penetrate for all the blackest corners on earth, through waves of the sea, to its caves of blue and corals; one as wounded eagle, as an ulcer on the chest looking like a rose, running away, to big moves of wings, up in the sky, with desperate and strident howls. In this way, as a spirit who is saying good-bye, Keleffy played the piano. He never did so much, nor had a second audience as such. For Sol was that fantasy; for Sol, to whom she would ever see again, nor would ever stop seeing. Only those who look for in vane pureness, know how satisfying and enhancing the act of finding it. Only those who died of love to beauty understand how, without bad thoughts, about to say good-bye forever to the friendly city, Keleffy played the piano that night. He played in such a way that even for uncultivated, that moment still an unforgettable. "He was leading us like a victorious" a commentarial said the next day, "in his car." Where we were going? Nobody knew it. A lightening on a mountain, as the steel of a giant on a castle where he supposed to have his enchanted lady; a lion with wings, going from cloud to cloud, a virgin sun in a fearful forest, as a serpent nest, rises up; a never seen corner of a forest, where trees had not leaves but flowers; a colossal pine with thunders and lamentations, it was breaking down; it as a great soul opening itself. The Hungarian had made everybody to admire him so much at the beginning of the celebration; however, that furious fantasy, that overflow of notes; whether as a lamenting woman paid to cry at funerals, as the terrible ones, they sounded like the story of a life, that one, the very last piece of the night, since nobody after her attempted to ask for another song, he came immediately after Miss Sol del Valle's appearance, the city was proud of her since all of us recognized the improvising of the pianist and the influence on him, as much influenced as those who saw her last night, on her white dress and her aureole of innocence, all these caused by the marvelous beauty of the girl. The unique beauty is well born, with the genius by her feet".

* * * * *

Two friends are seating under the shade of the Magnolia tree, our antique friend. On a chair is Lucia. Other Mimbre chairs wait for their owners, who are preparing candy in the house, or with Ana, who is not doing well today. She is so pale. No one from outside is expected this afternoon; Juan Jerez is not in the city: on Friday he went to defend at a tribunal of a neighbor town the rights of Indians children, to their lands, and he has not come back. Lucia would had been even sadder, if she did not have her friend by her side. Juan cannot come by. There is not train today. By horse, it is too far away. By Lucia's feet, on a little chair, with her arms crossed on the knees of the girl, who is the one seating and looks at her with long glances, that enter the soul as beautiful queens who are looking for into her bedroom, and to remain in herself; and she let her play with her head, which gray hair untied and revolt, and combs up later on, so carefully, in a way that her noble neck is seen? Sol del Valle is by Lucia's feet.

* * * * *

Since the night of Keleffy's party, Lucia and Sol had seen each other many times. By knowing her, as it happens in our cities where everybody knows one another, how come she could free herself of that? That one night, it was not actually Juan, Lucia, well adulated by the principal of La Merced Institute, where she had graduated three years before, saw herself in the arms of Sol, who saw her full of hope and tenderness. The principal did stand up and took Sol by her arm to the place where Lucia was, taciturn. She saw them coming, and she went backwards.

-They're coming towards me, towards me!-She told herself.

-Lucia, here am bringing a friend, just so you will put her in your heart, and you will take care of her for me, as a thing of your home. I may leave her in your hands: you are not envy.

The face of Sol would get turn on, without knowing what to say, and the color of Lucia would disappear, with no success on finding the strength to move her hand and opening her lips into a smile.

-This cannot be this way, not this way.

The principal put Sol arm on the hand of Lucia, having jealous glances, she took refuge with them for a few moments in a balcony, which granite gate was hidden under a clump of Solomonic roses. The balcony was huge and solemn; the night, already in advance, and the sky, lovely and loquacious, as it uses to turn in our countries when the air is clear, and it looks like the stars are visiting and talking.

-After all, Lucia and Sol, give each other a kiss.

-Look, Lucia-the principal said uniting in her hands the hands of the two girls talking and acting as Sol was not with them, who felt her cheeks burning, and the chest pressing with the things the teacher was telling, so much, that for an instant she saw the sky all black, as Doña Andrea was calling her from her little house-.Look, Lucia, you know Sol del Valle enters in life, as everybody knows. Her father has died. Her mother is in the worst of a poverty. Me, that I love her as a daughter, I have procured to educating her so she will save herself from the danger of being so beautiful but so poor.

Lucia felt in that instant as if Sol hand was trembling in hers, and she had made a move to take it away and standing herself up.

-Mrs...

-No, no, Lucia. The one who will be Juan Jerez gentlewoman...

The shadow of one of the curtains in the clump that floated on the influence of the air, hiding in this moment the face of Sol.

-...deserves that I put in his hands, so he will show her by his side to the world, and he will protect her, the jewel of the house to whom Juan Jerez has been so kind.

Here the floating curtain of the clump covered with its shadow the face of Lucia.

-Juan...

-Juan has been so gentle-she said with certain sense of a conscious hurry to the principal-. he just knows Sol, since he has visited so little the house of Doña Andrea; but he is so generous, will be so happy for you taking care of this girl, with the respect of your house, of those, since they will see her unprotected...

Whiter than her dress one could see the face of Sol in this moment.

-...they would want to disrespect her. Sol has already finish her studies; in order to complete my work, I am going to leave her on it as a teacher, so she will support her mother taking care of the house, we have already taken a house for Doña Andrea near the Institute. I hope-the lady added indeed, as the stars were not shinning in the sky-, Sol will be a great teacher. I, Lucia, will not be able to take her everywhere, since am no longer young, and the duties of studies stop me from doing it; but I want you to do my ways, you already know that-she said with a light emotion on her voice giving Lucia a kiss on her cheek-, take care of her for me. They would feel the one cannot reach you, would not reach her either. Whenever there is a party, take her to it. She will always dress so beautiful, since I have taught her to do everything, and she is a master in weaving. Invite her to your house, so no one would have excuses for not inviting her to theirs: the one who enters to your house, could enter anywhere else. Sol is as beautiful as thankful.

-Yes, yes, Madam-Lucia interrupted whom was feeling on her cheeks the same ones paleness as those of Sol-. I will take her with me. Of course, I will, I will introduce her to all my friends right away. We will go together this Eastern. Do not refuse to it, Sol. We will go to the theatre always together.

Love was growing up with the words, she was telling rapidly, as if she was in a hurry to forget something, or she wanted to take revenge of herself.

-Well, let´s go then, I see people are curious because we are gossiping for such a long time. Let´s go.

-Right away, Mrs. right away. Get in first and we will go after you. I will take two roses of this clump: this one for Sol-and she put it on her so much tenderness, looking at her with love into her eyes-;this one, which is less wonderful, for me.

-Oh, you are so kind!

-You? No, Sol, I am your sister. Do not pay attention what the principal says. I will always love you as a sister-she did open her arms, and hugged in hers the arms of Sol, whom she was holding fearless, very firmly.

-Oh!-Sol said soon drowning a howl. She took her arm to her chest, and took it with the tip of her bleeding fingers. Due the hug with Lucia, a thorn of the rose did hurt her chest.

With her own handkerchief Lucia dried the blood, and holding hands the two of them entered the living room. Lucia was looking beautiful as well.

* * * * *

-How someone could understand you, Lucia?-Juan told her cousin about fifteen days before the night of the party, with a severe intention into the words that he had never used towards Lucia-. Since fifteen days ago, wait, I believe I remember, since the night of Keleffy, I find you so unfair, that sometimes, I think you do not love me.

-Juan! Juan!

-Well, Lucia: you love me indeed. What did I do to cause this hardness of heart of your character, what will explain your cruelty, for me whom is coming to you as the thirsty comes to a glass of tenderness? You cannot be wishing more love. Thinking, I do think of the most difficult and the boldest one; loving, Lucia, I love nobody but you. I have lived just a little; am afraid to live and I know what that is, since I look at the ones who are alive. It looks to me that everyone is stained, as when one reaches to see a pure man they start running behind him to staining his tunic of blemishes. Truth is I, whom appreciates gentlemen so much, I live my life escaping from them. I often feel a painful melancholy. What else can happens to myself? Fortune has treated me well. My parents live for me. For me, it is allow to be good. Plus, I have you-he told her while holding her hand, in such a lovely manner that Lucia moved her hand of as being embarrassed and amazed.

-I posses you, from you it is coming, I look for into yourself, the fresh force that I need to keep my heart from weakness and astonishment. Every time I see gentlemen, I turn myself backwards as if I was seeing a depth, every time I come by to see you, I acquire the brightness to battle and a power to forgive that make nothing difficult for me so I can accomplish them. Quit laughing Lucia; it is the truth. You have read verses by Longfellow entitled "Excelsior"? A young fellow on a tempest of ice, climbs on a poor seaport, up the mountain, with a flag on his hand that says: "Excelsior". Do not laugh: I know you know your Latin: "Higher!". An old fellow tells him not to continue on, that the torrent is howling downhill and the tempest is coming over!: Higher!". A beautiful young lady, not as beautiful as you!, tells him: "Let your fatigued head resting on my chest". and the blue eyes of the young fellow get moisture, but he puts apart from him the in-love-lady and tells her: "Higher!".

-Oh, no! You will not put myself apart of you. Am taking the flag of your hands. You are staying with me. I am the highest!

-No, Lucia: the two of us will hold the flag. Am taking you for the entire journey. Look that, since am kind, I will not be happy. Don't you get tired!-and he kissed her hand.

Lucia was caressing with her eyes his head.

-The young man finally kept moving on: the monks found him dead the next day, half buried in snow; holding the flag in his hand, the one that says: "Higher!". Well, Lucia: when you're not getting yourself difficult, when you don't do the things you did to me yesterday, you saw me up front with a hateful look and you did laugh of me and of my kindness, without knowing it you did even doubt of my honesty, when you don't get crazy as yesterday, it seems to me when am leaving this place, the flag is shinning in my hands. I see the whole world so small, and I see myself as a joyful giant. I feel greater need, a vehement need of loving and forgiving the entire world. In the gentlewoman, Lucia, as she is the greatest beauty one knows, we the poets believe we find in herself as a natural perfume all the existences of spirit; that is way the poets attach themselves with such passion to women whom they love, specially to the first one to whom they really love, who is not normally they first one they had believe they love, that is why when they believe a childish or unconsidered act disfigure them, or they imagine some emptiness or impureness, they get out of their minds, and mortal pains are felt, they treat their lovers with such an indignation as they would treat thieves and traitors, since in their minds they made their gentlewomen depositaries of all their greatness and clarities they wished for, when they believe the do not have them, they think their gentlewomen have been stealing and cheating on them with refined wickedness, they believe they are tumbling down as a broken mount, by the earth, they die although they continue living, hugging the fallen leaves of their white rose. Foremost poets die. Second rank poets, the lieutenants and lieutenancies; of poetry, the falsified poets, continue their way for the world kissing in revenge as much lips as they can, with theirs, reds and wets in what it is seem, but what it is not seem red in venom! Come on, Lucia, today you are making me a great speaker. You see, I can´t help it. If other people did hear me, they would say I was a pedant. You´re not saying that, right? What happens is while am close to you, close to you whom no one has stained, close to you whom no one has put his impure lips, from you I measure as the flesh of all my ideas and as a pillow of stars where I recline, when no one sees me, the fatigued head, these strange things, Lucia, come to my lips so naturally that the false one it would be not remembering them. In the outside they tend to accuse me of being exaggerated, of being a real snob, and you may already noticed I talk so little. It is not my fault that my nature is this type, not my fault of showing all my flowers due the influence of your tenderness?

He kissed both of her hands, as a child could had kissed two doves.

There, even when it does not sound truth, some human beings tend to talk in this way "alive and affectionate", as the head-stones where military officers who died on duty of the Spanish Crown. In this way, exactly, without taking of or adding apices, it was the way Juan Jerez felt and talked.

    * * * * *

-Do you forgive me, Juan-Lucia said before a few moments had passed, under the eyes and the voice, as the one of a contrite sinner who is humble asking for the absolution of his sin-. Juan I don´t know what it is, neither I know what for I love you, even though I know that I love you for the same reason I live, if I did not love you I was not living. Look, Juan, am lying to you; right now am lying to you, I believe I don´t know why I love you, I shall know it quite well, without myself noticing it, because I know why the rest of them must love you. Since they know you, they must love you as much as I do, don´t you grumble me Juan! I wished you knew nobody! I would love you voiceless, I would love you blind: so would not see other but me, I would close the steps to the world, I would be always there, as inside of you, by your feet where I wanted to be right now! Do you forgive me Juan? Then, am not arrogant, I don't think am just beauty: you say am beautiful! I know that besides me there are many things and many beautiful and great people; I know that I don't posses all the beauties of earth, all of them fit in your heart, you are so tender that I had seen you picking up the smashed flowers down the streets and carefully putting where nobody step on them, I believe, Juan, that am not enough for you, that whoever beautiful thing or person, would like you so much as I do, I hate a book if you read it, I hate a friend if you visit him, I hate a woman if they say she is beautiful and you might see her. I wish to unite in myself all the beauties of the world, I wished nobody else but me had beauty on earth. Because I love you, Juan, I hate it all. Am not bad, Juan; I am ashamed of that, then I feel remorse, I would kiss the feet of those who moments ago I wanted to see dead, I would give them of my blood so they would live if they had died; there are instants, Juan, where I hate everything, all men and all women! Oh, I hate all women! When you're not by my side, I think of someone who could gratify your eyes or occupy your thought, believe me, Juan; I don't even know what I see, I don't even know what possesses me, you horrify me, Juan and I abhor you then, I hate your very same qualities, I set them on your face, like yesterday, just to see if you reached the point of hating them, if it is not so good, if they do not love you still! That's it, Juan, it is not more than that. Sometimes, I will say it to you only, I suffer so much that I lie on the floor in my room, when no one sees me, like a dead one. I need to feel on my temples for so long the coldness of marble. I get myself up, as if my insides were all broken into pieces. I die of an enormous envy for all the things you can believe in as well as all those who could love you. I don't know whether that is bad, Juan: Can you forgive me?

The magnolia, our good old friend did hear, by the last lights of that evening, the end of this distressing conversation.

* * * * *

Pretty is the mount that dominates the East side of the city, where strong arms fought back in the day, flint against lance and flesh against iron, the chief of the Indians and the chief of the Castilians, and from cliff to cliff fighting, killing and admiring each other they were falling, till finally, exhaust, hurting himself with his own flint his head, the Indian felt down to the feet of the Spanish one, who moved his eye protector, letting see his face all cover by blood, kissed the dead Indian on his hand. Then, as it was hard to climb, they choose it for their penitence the devotes, it is a famous thing that for its rocky declivity they did climb on their knees during the hardest of the sun, the penitents, counting the rosary.

New people came in, as the mount is short and of a pretty shape, from it the city is seen, with its low houses, with trees in backyards, as a great basket of garlands and opals, they cleaned it up of stones and weeds the manure land, resulted grateful; from the best part of the mount they planted a garden which has no rival among the cities in America, since it is not just a little-pity garden of weak flowers, with pruned bushes, with little pieces of leaves between bob wire fences, that more than anything else they give the impression of slavery and artifice, discreet and good people walk away from them; but one as a forest of our lands, with our own great flowers and our fruit trees, they are there showing willingness with such an art with grace and abandon, in irregular groups and as few citizens, in such a way it does not look like those bamboos, plantains and orange trees have been brought there by the hands of the gardener, neither those water lilies planted there as a bunch embroidering the edge of the narrow creek full of dried waters, they have been transplanted there as in fact they were: well before, it looks like all that flourished there due its own and free well, in such a way that the soul pleases itself and communicates fearless, when a person from the city is happy, he needs to climb the dear mount who is never by itself, neither at nights nor at days.

Over there, during he afternoon when we are walking, Pedro Real found a reason to go by horse, he let it on the top, meanwhile, hitting his boots with a small whip, was getting lost, without remembering Ana´s painting, on the lily street. Over there, without even knowing that Pedro was near by, Adela had just, with three friends of hers, who were just wearing brand new straw hats decorated with lilies, had just got of the wagon that was waiting on top with the horses. Over there, Adela did not even know either, even though Pedro knew it, they were slowly, with the younger girls, Sol and Doña Andrea: Doña Andrea, since school had given back to her Sol and she now could recreate her eyes, with certain shame of seeing in her soul a little soft and lazy, in that little girl of her of a "such as transparent face-she said-as a cloud that I saw once in Paris, in a center site in Murillo", she was always talking to herself in low voice, as she was praying; and other times she was grumbling for everything, she the one who never grumble, since she really loved him, without being audacious, was lying to Sol, from whom she would turn into a jealous and fears attack, every time she heard one preparing for a party or going for an outing, which were not much by the way, but fair enough for justifying the fears of Doña Andrea for her treasure. Not even the greatest wellbeing, nor the great salary she saved during the time Sol had come back from school, those things were not enough for Doña Andrea; and some times a big injustice occurred; the beauty she babysit the most, she took care of the girl since she was little, she favored her, she would claim it as a mere sin, that made her one day to say such a curious absurdity which was taken for some people as gracious as right: "If Manuel was alive, you would not be so beautiful". Doña Andrea got upset, when she heard, when Sol was coming back from school with an old mistress, the bold steps of the horse of certain gentleman to whom she specially hated; and if Sol had showed, which she never did, desires to see the arrogant mount, besides one time she saw smiling and not discontent, to see it passing by behind some windows, it is for sure Doña Andrea would have feel her bitterness, who was looking at that magnanimous gallant, to Pedro Real, as seeing an abominable enemy. Doña Andrea would have stand not even one gallant, which concerns increased the certitude that the one she had loved for having him in her soul, that one who possessed her Sol, would never belong to Sol, due the highness she was at, since her was someone else´s. That such an honest lady would trembled when thought that, for seeing well proportioned in the great external beauty, might get close in loves that taster of vivid lips and that cup of new wine. Doña Andrea felt virile forces, as well as determination to employ them, every time the horse of Pedro Real stepped on the bricks of the street. As the bodies show the soul that they carry inside! Once, in a room full of nacre, a bandit was found taking refuge. It is horrible seeing so many smart and handsome men. One runs away, as from a burrow. It was well known around the whole city, with envy of many frivolous ones, behind Sol del Valle, Pedro Real had thrown all his desires, his melodic eyes, his strong figure, his caracoling horses, his impetus of a legendary lover. The despotic of the fanaticism was known by, rudely, as he had not being perturbing with his glimmers of love his new souls, he ceased of saying gallantries, to affect disdains to those who were closer to him since his arrival from Paris, whether because they were publicly considered as the most wanted conquests, or due the hotness of his treatment given to his easy occasion so those salt-and-pepper conversations which are not that frequent among young gentlemen of us who have seen lands, fill up with the speech the lack of grace and intellect. The conversation with the gentlewomen has to be one of fine silver, worked in light filigrees, as they work it both in Geneva and Mexico.

If seen where Sol del Valle had to see him, Pedro Real did put the greatest attention; no one could see her if he was not seen either; if in theater, under the balcony where Sol went, the one that was the principal's, no more than twice, there was the pit of the play-house, there was Pedro at the lunette; whether on Eastern, where Sol went with Lucia and Adela, Pedro, with no mercy for Adela, appeared. Telling her, he had tell her nothing. Neither writing her. No one affected him, by saluting her in public, greater resignation and moderation. He looked more arrogant, since he was not so beautified. Neither he told her, nor he wrote her; he wanted to fill up her air with himself. While leaving the theatre, the second night he approached Sol, a little child with pita hat and barefoot was offering a clump of Camellias of red color, which were there so much expensive and appreciated. By the time Sol left, in such a rapid way that to everyone looked like an artistic thing, Pedro Real took the clump, he destroyed it in a way that the Camellias were falling on the ground, almost to the feet of Sol, said, as he did not want to be heard only by the friend by his side: "Since these cannot be of the right person, so they will not belong to someone at all". As the fantasy that Sol beauty took away from Keleffy was already a manner of legend in the city, Pedro Real, with greater and deeper tact one could suppose of him, he bought it, so no one could ever played on it, the piano where that night Sol and Keleffy had played.

* * * * *

The oboes were happily playing in the city, as well as the fifes and drums. The balconies on the Victory Street were baskets of roses, with all the girls and gentlewomen of the city looking at them. For each entry on the Victory Street, with its band of little drums leading, a company of militia members appeared. One of them wearing white drilling trousers, with short, pearl like-wool and loose jackets, the chest crossed by wide white-belts, with silver flagstaff. Others were wearing in red and white, white the trouser, the jacket in red. Others more of citizens, although less brilliant ones, more virile ones: wearing dark blue trousers, one like a short overcoat, just fastened with double lines of gold buttons in front: the hat was made of black felt and wide wings, with a light cord of gold, hanging with two acorns to their backs. The battalions were taking their places in the corners. How touching the tearing flags! How arrogant like priest looking, those who were carrying them! They looked tall even though they were not. They did not look well, near by those disreputable pavilions, the little silk flags and golden flowers where the numbers of the battalions were embroidered with embossing letters. How anxiously the boys ran on the streets! It is the truth even grown men, newspaper in hand and cane in the air, all were running. In the eyes of some of them tears were seen. It appeared something pushed the people from the inside. When a band was playing in the distance, as it was leaving, boys, even the fullest grown, ran behind it, with their anguished faces, as if life was running away from them. The smallest ones, going from one side to the other, they were seen from the balconies, they looked like grapes apart of a clump. It was around nine in the morning, the sky was happy, as it was all right for it what was going on in the earth. It was that day of the year to bring flowers to the sepulchers of soldiers who died defending the independence of the motherland. Between a battalion and the other, enormous wagons were in the procession, pulled by white horses, staves with abundant flowers in them. In the cemetery there was a flag nailed in every sepulcher.

Who was the only gentleman among the most elegant ones in the city, who was not that morning, with a clump of flowers in the buttonhole, saluting the ladies and girls from his horse? The students, no, those were not in the streets, although they were hanging out with their sisters and girl friends in the balconies: the students were at the procession, all dressed in black, between admirers and envy ones of the dead soldiers they were visiting, since these ones, had already died in defense of their motherland, but they did not yet: they saluted their sisters and girl friends in the balconies, as they were saying good bye the them. The mass of students went to honor the dead soldiers. Students are the bulwark of Freedom and its firmest army. Universities seem to be useless, but from there martyrs and apostles graduated. In that city, who was the one ignoring when a freedom was in danger, when a newspaper was threaten, when votes of suffrage were at risk, students got together, dressed to a party like, with their heads uncovered and holding hands, they went on the streets asking for justice; or they gave ink to the press in a basement, the printed what they could not say; the gathered in the ancient Alameda, when the professors wanted to brake down their honor, out of a trunk they made a chair for the best of them, for the one they named the professor, love for trees, through such branches the sky looked like a subtle embroidered, set on books he said with enthusiasm his lessons; whether in silence, challenging death, pales as angels, together as brothers, they entered on the street that went to the public house where they had to deposit their votes, once the Government did not want people to vote other than its attendant ones, they started falling one by one, without going backward, the ones going on the others, the chest and heads passed through by bullets, those bullets letting be shot by the soldiers in abundant discharges? That day Juan Jerez did remain safe by a marvelous event, because an uncle of Pedro Real leaded off the rifle of a soldier who was aiming at him. That is why, when students were passing on the procession, dressed in black, with a yellow flower in the button hole, the handkerchiefs of all the balconies were let to the wind, men would take their hat off in the street, as when the flags were passing; the girls used to take off their chest the clumps of roses and throwing them on the students.

In a balcony, with her two older sisters and the principal, there was Sol del Valle. In another one, with a dress that would make her looking like a silver image, a beautiful pagan sculpture, there was Adela. Further, where Sol and Adela could see her, was occupying a wide balcony, covered from the sun by a tent of sailcloth, there were Lucia with several members of the family of her mother, and Ana. On a chair with arms Ana had been brought to the house. She was so sick, without her knowing it well; she was doing really bad. She wanted to see, "with her right of an artist, that celebration of colors; earth was lacking of color, and it is not that right Juan? Look, if not, how come everybody is wearing in black. I want to listen to the music, Lucia: I want to listen to music so much. I want to see the flags in the wind". There she was in the wide balcony, dressed in white, very sheltered, as the weather was so cold, looking avariciously, as she feared not see again what she was seeing, feeling inside her chest, so no one could see them, tears where falling over it.

Lucia distinguished Sol, she looked whether she was in the balcony, or Juan Jerez was inside. Sol, not fairly good saw Lucia, she never her eyes off her, so she would notice she was there, when she thought Lucia was looking at her, saluted her in a lovely way with her hand, with the smile and the eyes at the same time. She preferred Lucia was the one looking at her, instead of the boys best known in the city, those young men who always found a way to stop more than natural in front of her balcony. Pedro Real received a move of her head after his humble salute, when he passed by on his horse; she did not see him with embarrassment, she did not see him with affection either so she would not worry Doña Andrea, Adela saw such things from her balcony, although she was facing in the other direction. Lucia had entered by the soul of Sol, since the evening when she felt a joy after the thorn of the rose was nailed in her chest. Lucia, ardent and despotic, sometimes submissive as one who is in love, rigid and frenetic right away with no apparent cause, beautiful then as a red rose, she exercised, since she did not wish it for, a powerful influence on the spirit of Sol, shy and new. Sol was someone to be taking by the hand during life, better prepared by Nature to be loved rather than giving love, she was happy since those near by her were not, not because a especial generosity, but for certain inability of hers being neither so venturous nor so unfortunate. She had the enchant of white roses. An owner was required for her, Lucia was her owner.

Lucia had come to see her; to look for her in her wagon so they would take an outing together; so Ana would go to her house to know it; Ana wanted to make a painting of it; Lucia refused to it "because now Ana was fatigued, she would paint when she was stronger", all these being said by Lucia, made sense to Sol. Lucia went to dress her one evening when Sol went to the theatre, and she did not go: Why she did not go? Juan Jerez did not go that evening either; by the way Lucia brought her that evening a collar of pearls so she could wear it: "No one has seen it on me, Sol: I never wear pearls"; however, Doña Andrea, who had started giving signs of sharpness and unusual integrity, she took Lucia by hands when she was offering the collar to Sol, who did not see a sin by wearing it, looking at the eyes of the friend of her daughter, and tightening her hand with tenderness and firmness at the same time, she told her with an accent she let quite few doubts: "No, my little girl, no", what Lucia understood very well, the collar of pearls remained as forgotten. Next morning, at the time Sol went to her classes, Lucia went to look for her so they could go for an outing by the school, she asked her with painful and over exalted eagerness, who she had seen, who went up her box seat, who caught the attention to her, where Pedro Real was at: "Oh! Pedro Real, such a good gentleman; don´t you like Pedro Real? I believe Pedro Real would get the attention everywhere. Have you noticed since Pedro Real meet you how he does not care about anybody but you"; Lucia quit talking about these things quite soon. Who was the one at the theatre, she did not care about knowing it very much: Juan was not there; who was at the exit? Don´t you remember who was at the exit? Was...? She just had asked who was there. Neither Sol knew whom she was asking for. No: Sol saw anybody. She was going very happy. The principal had treated her with so much love. Yes, Pedro Real had been there; he did not went to say hello to her: nobody went up to say hello to her. They had looked at her so much though. They said the French consul had said a very pretty thing about her. While leaving theater, no, she saw nobody. Sol wanted to arrive soon, since doña Andrea was sad when they had departed. When they got to the school with this conversation, Lucia kissed Sol with such coldness, so the girl stopped herself for a moment looking at her with the painful eyes, those eyes that did not bother the front head of her friend. Suddenly, during many days, Lucia quit seeing her. Sol had become afflicted, doña Andrea did not: although she was proud of everyone loving her daughter; Lucia did not: she never saw Lucia in a kind manner. A day before the procession Lucia had returned to the house of Sol. Asking her for forgiveness. Ana was so lonely. Sol was so more beautiful than ever before. "Look, tomorrow I will send you the most beautiful Camellia I have at home. Am not telling you to come to my balcony, because... I know you´re going to the principal´s balcony". Look, you are going to be so beautiful; place the Camellia on your head, on the right side, so I can see it on you from my balcony". She hold her hands, and kissed them; while she talked to Sol, she passed her hand softly on her cheek; when she told her good bye, she saw her as she knew a danger was going on, as she was warning her about it, when she walked to the horse wagon, tears were already rolling from her eyes.

-There she is, there she is!-she said involuntarily, rejecting right away to herself for what she had said, one of the sisters of Sol, the oldest one, the one who was not beautiful, the one who had nothing but two very black and charming eyes, expressive and sweets as those of the alpaca, the animal who die when one talks to it with cruelty.

-Who?

-Was nobody: Juan Jerez, in Lucia´s balcony.

-Yes, I see him already. Lucia, he is looking at here-and he fastened and unfastened from the car, so Lucia would noticed him, so she would believe he thought of her-.Little sister-Sol said suddenly in low voice-;little sister, don´t you think Juan Jerez is so kind? I would love to see him more. I never see him when I go visit at Lucia's house. I don't know what he has, it seems to me he is the best. You think he loves Lucia so much?

Little sister didn't want to say a word, she pretended not to listen one thing.

-Juan Jerez used to come home sometimes, before I got out of school; right? Tell me, since you're the one who knows him. I know he will marry Lucia, although she never tells me thing about him; I love talking things about him. Am not brave enough to ask Lucia things about him, since she does not tell me... He's been so kind with my mom, right? The principal loves him so much! Look, over there is Pedro Real again: he's really such a kind gentleman! I find strange eyes on him, they're not as sweet as Juan's. I don't know, but the evening of Keleffy the only one who told me something, I have not forgotten, that one was Juan Jerez.

Little sister did not say a word. Her eyes had turned so black, so wide open as if she was holding something on them.

She, was not looking at the balcony, she was afraid Juan Jerez had been keeping his eyes on the kind Sol for such a long time. Juan, the one who charmed the marbles, the one who followed the barefoot boys on the streets until he knew where they lived, the one who took the flowers from the floor so no one could step on them, when nobody saw him, he would comb their petals, he would put them in safe place. In the same way, with the same honest deceit that produces in a fine spirit the contemplation of beauty, Juan had been looking at Sol for so long.

Then, Lucia was not there. Poor Ana! When the last soldiers were passing by, she turned pale, sweat covered her face, and she closed her eyes and felt on her knees. They carried her inside, to make her sense coming back. She looked like a saint, dressed in white, with her face all yellow. Lucia stayed by her side; Ana had awaked; Lucia had looked at the door many times, as wondering where Juan would be. "In the balcony? I hope he´s not there in the balcony!". Ana still dismayed, she almost abandoned her hand.

-Go, go with Juan!-Ana told her, she barely opened her eyes, she noticed her calamity; with her hand and smile she sent her to the door in a softly way.

-Well, well, I´ll be right back.

She went to the balcony right away.

-Juan!

-How is Ana? How is she doing?

The balcony of the principal was already empty.

-She is fine: she is doing well. I did not know where you were!

* * * * *

Now we come back to the feet of the Magnolia, when so many days have passed after all these things happened, Sol was on a stool by the feet of Lucia who was sitting on an iron chair. Ana, with her capricious of a mother, wanted them to bring Sol to her. "She is so kind, Lucia! You shall not be afraid of her, you are beautiful as well. Look: I see beautiful people as if they were sacred. When they´re bad, no: they seem to me as Japanese glasses full of mud; as long as they are good, don´t you laugh, it seems to me, when am in front of them, I am a monastic student and am lifting the cowl to a priest as during mass. Come on, bring Sol here; is it really that Juan isn´t coming today?".

-That´s the truth! Yes, yes; am going there right now, I´ll bring Sol for you.

Sol Came, as well as other friends of Ana, Adela did not. Ana was living on chair for sick ones, walking was embarrassing for her, she could not recline herself. As when the light if going off, she had her face clear and confused at the same time, all of it as showered by a sweet kindness. She had not wishes, she wished so little from earth while she was on it, what Ana should ask the earth, it was sure was not on it, perhaps it was out of it. Neither Ana felt death, it did not seem like death what was increasing inside herself, it was more like an ascension. She must see such beautiful things, as she was dying, without noticing she was seeing them, since they were a reflection on her front face. She had the fore head as wax looking, high and burnished, the walls of her temples had a sinking looking. Those eyes were a pledge. Her nose was fine, like a line. The lips irritated and dried, they were like a source of forgiveness. She did not said but charities. Alone, she did not want to be by herself. Nobody wants to be alone when entering into a journey: neither when one is close to a wedding. It is the unknown, therefore the fearful one. One looks for the companion of those who love us. Ana had so much love for others, during her illness, she even feel more love for Sol, whom perfect beauty was greater, if it does fit, due the innocent interest and thoughts the little girl had for her. Ana was doing better when holding Sol by her hand, in which hours Lucia, seating by them, was so kind.

Ana was sleeping in those moments, while Lucia and Sol were talking by the piano. They talked about school, she had taken the exam that week, she was leaving Sol alone for two months: Sol did not enjoy teaching that much, no, "Of course I enjoy it: don´t you understand in this way mom is not in troubles? Mom!". Sol was telling these things to Lucia, without noticing that this one was frowning, how uncomfortable the cares by Pedro Real would turn doña Andrea, the gentle lady talked about everything else, so the girl would not put her eyes on him; but she did not, she did not think about that.

-No, why not?

-I don´t know, I don´t think about that yet; I like it, yes, I like the way he takes care of me; I like better coming over here, or when you go there to see me, being with Ana and with you. Then, Pedro Real scares me. When he sees me, it looks he does not love me. I don´t know how to explain it, it looks to me he wants another thing in myself, a thing is not my own. That is how it seems to me, come on, Lucia, you can tell me that! It seems to me that when a man loves us, we should see us into his eyes, as we were in them, the two times I have seen Pedro Real from a short distance, it did not seem to me finding myself in his eyes. It is not the truth, Lucia, when some one loves one it does happen that way?

In the hand of Lucia the Sol´s hair got curled while playing.

-Ay! You´re hurting me.

-You want us to go see how´s Ana?

She was standing up to go see her, fixing up her hair, that fine hair, blond with golden reflexes, when at the same time two different noises were heard: one in Ana´s room, as the one of a crowd moving and talking loudly, the other one by the door by the street, where, with disembarrassed air, a handsome man jumped off a road mule.

-Juan!-Lucia murmured, turning whiter than the Camellias.

-Juan Jerez?-Sol said turning her face happy, just completing on getting her braids tied.

Lucia, standing up and frowning, with her eyes on Sol, who was feeling disturbed by that silence, she awaited holding the iron chair, looking at Juan, he was just taking a glance at Sol, he was coming towards his cousin with his hands open.

-Ms. Sol, what you´ve done to my Lucia? Why don´t you walk to receive me? Just to punish me since to come see you today I have been riding twenty-two leagues on mule´s back?

Lucia´s lips were unnoticeably shaking and her eyes were getting wide open. Her hand was shaking in Juan´s hands, he was looking at her with astonishment.

Sol pretended she was fixing the flowers of a glass on a little table.

-Lucia, what´s wrong?

-Sol, Lucia, come over here!-said while approaching them a friend of theirs who was exiting Ana's room abruptly-. Ah, Juan, it is so nice of you being here. Go, Lucia, go, I believe Ana is dying.

-Ana!

-Yes, send some one for a doctor right away.

Juan jumped off the mule and started walking so fast. Sol was besides Ana already, Lucia saw slowly to the street door, she looked with anger the door where Sol had entered, she remained standing up for a few moments, alone at the patio, her two quite arms, compressed to the sides, her eyes firm in front of her in a tenacious way. She started walking towards Ana's room after looking everywhere as if she was afraid.

* * * * *

To the field! To the field! All of them are going to the field. All, yes, all of them. Adela and Pedro Real, Lucia and Juan, Ana and Sol. Of course, the older people who will not have an influence on this narrative do not figure on it. To the field all!

The doctor arrived that Sunday in moments when Ana was opening her eyes, Sol on her knees by the edge of the bed was the first image they saw.

-Ah, you, Sol!-Sol was passing her hand on the fore head, she was moving her wet hair from it.

Lucia was fixing the pillows in such a way Ana could be like seating. All her friends were surrounding the bed, Ana, without the strength even to talk, was paying their anguished looks with recognizing ones. It looked she was joyful. Sol wanted to take off the hand where she was holding Ana´s; Ana stopped her.

-What happened, uh, what happened? I felt like a whole building had been demolished inside of me. It is over, it´s over. Am well now. Her felt on the other side of the pillows.

The doctor found her in this way, he put his hear on her heart, open the doors and windows from pair to pair and advice that only the one she wishes will stay there right next to her.

Ana, who seems not to hear, open her eyes, as the air was doing so goon on her said:

-Juan has arrived, Lucia.

-How did you know?

-Go with Juan, Lucia. Sol, you stay here.

Sol looked at Lucia, as wondering; to Lucia, who was standing by the bed, hard her lips and her arms loose.

Juan was knocking on the door at that instant, the doctor lead him by the hand to the room.

-Come tell me rather is not of crazies thinking this handsome girl is at risk-with the eyes, the doctor was unsaying his own words-. It is indispensable the little ill girl go sees the countryside. It is indispensable. Don´t you ask me what remedy she needs-the doctor saying putting his eyes on Juan-. A lot of rest, much of fresh air, much of smell of trees. Take her where there is heat, this humid weather could cause much damage on her. If you´re able to depart tomorrow, the journey could begin tomorrow. Don´t you go alone girl. Take people who love you, people who shelter you at mornings and evenings. And this gentle girl?-he added turning to Sol-. I think you'll get well if you take with you this gentle girl.

-Oh, yes, Sol is going with me; right Juan?

-Of course-Juan said vividly, thinking with pleasure that Ana would rejoice herself, whom love for Sol was already well known, a task of love would be given to the poor widow-: of course we will take her. It will a whole gala for the eyes to see them going on roses path that I know, holding hands, Sol, Ana and Lucia. Lucia, we're leaving tomorrow. Sol, right now am going to your house to ask doña Adela for permission. Do you agree, Lucia, if we invite Adela and Pedro Real? Oh, Ana, ah! I have my little Indian friends over there in that village that will give you reasons for a beautiful painting. Want to go with us, doctor?-Juan charmed a hand of Ana and kissed Lucia's, with a kiss that was sweetly grumbling her and exit to the corridor, talking to the doctor as very content.

Ana called Lucia with a glance, so she got next to her, without saying a word, smiling happily, she took on her chest with an effort the hands of Lucia and Sol's, they were on each of her side and moving her eyes on their heads, like she was talking to them, hold both hands of both girls under hers for a long time.

Sol looked at Lucia in such a pretty way and Ana felt asleep, Lucia approached Sol, took her by her waist in a charming way, once in her room, started empty with moves almost febrile her boxes and drawers.

-Everything, everything is for you-Sol wanted to talk and she would not let her-. Look, try this hat on. I have never wear it. Try it on, put it on. This one, that one. Those three are yours. Yes, yes, don´t say no. Look, dresses: one, two, three. This one is the most beautiful for you. You heard me? I love Pedro Real so much. I want you to love Pedro Real. So he will see you so handsome. So they will see you prettier than me. Listen, do not love Juan. You let Juan be for my own. Make him feel angry. Treat him bad. I don´t want you to be his friend. No, don´t say a word! Yes, it is a joke, a joke. See? This Mallows dress will fit you so good. Let´s see, how great goes with your blond hair. You see? It is so new. It has the bodice as the chalice of a flower, a little bit straight; not like those of these days, that look like a glass of Champagne, so narrow on the waist, so wide on the shoulders. The dress skirt is so smooth, has no hammer bars looking nor wrinkles; it falls with the weight of the silk down to the feet. You see? It is too short for me. For you it will be all right. It is a little wide, kind of Watteau´s. My little shepherd girl! I have never wore them. You know? I don´t like light colors. Oh! Look: here you are-she was hiding something in her hands behind her back-, here you are, and you will never take them off, even though doña Andrea got upset with us. Close your eyes.

Sol closed her eyes venturous for being so loved by her friend, when she open her eyes, saw on her arm and attempted to take off with a gesture that Lucia stopped, a bracelet of four margarita-pearl rings.

-Yes, yes, it is very expensive; I want you to own it. No: nothing, do not say a word: see? Here I have another one, one of black pearls. Never, ever take it off you! I want to be so kind-and she took her by her hands, kissed her on her cheeks with passion-. Come, let's see Ana!

They left the room, holding each other waist.

To the field, to the field! Doña Andrea does not know Pedro Real is going; if she knew it, she would not allow Sol to go: although Juan what should she deny to him? To Juan! That one, he was the one she would want for Sol. "Well, Juan: don't let her staying in the sun that much". Juan asked with no success for the older sister, for Little sister. She was in the house when he entered; but not now: she may be at some neighbor house. No, Little sister was there; she was at the dining room, behind the venetian blinds! She saw the one who did not see her. "Close your eyes, Little sister, don't look at what you should not!". When Juan left, the venetian blinds closed like eyes.

To the field, to the field! For mules are pulling the car, with silver collars and bells, so Ana will go happy: the mules wear a great red crests on their left haunch, they look well on their black skin. The coachman is Pedro Real, whom is riding with Adela by his side, on the imperial, Juan and Lucia, inside, with the older people, who are very respectable, but they're not needed for the plot of the novel, Ana is seating among pillows, much better with the joy of the journey, with her notebook on her skirt, to copy what she like about the road, she believe it is well, Sol by her side, wearing a silk dress with opal color, tranquil and resplendent as a star.

Pedro Real bite his curled mustache when realized Sol was not going to be his partner on the coach-box. He was very gentle to Adela. You think Ana needs something, Juan? You think she going all right? We should stop. Will stop for a moment, to see if Ana is all right! He went down for many moments. The mules, although skillful, more than once they got off the road, as a sign the mind of the coach driver was not really on them.

The road was around six leagues long, all of it on one side and the other with such abundant vegetation that one could not avoid having his eyes with the constant gift and movement. Over there at the end there was whether a forest with coconut trees, or faraway palm trees that was leading to the throat of two mounts; it was whether to the merge of the road, a slope full of yellow and blue flowers that end into a river of white foams, fed by the waters of the mountains, or they were at the distance, imposing as two messages from earth to sky, two dormant volcanoes, which declivity with serpent looking the small springs and creeks of white, playful and living water would get together as wiped serfs by the feet of his masters, the antique cities, toothless and broken, in which balconies of decorated iron, kept by miracles without walls on the stone doors, there were growing in lines that would reach the ground in copious twining plants of Ipomoea. Up from a church that had the roof painted, the spire of the pillars in golden of fine gold, the oldest one in America, remained standing, like a shell nailed on the ground for its edge, the deepness of the major altar, covered by a half sepulcher: a small forest had grown to the love of the altar; the interior wall, covered with moss, would give an appearance from the distance of a formidable cave; it was a common thing and greatly nice seeing how from the flowering rocky places, while the minor noise of people of cars, a pack of doves. Other church, that did not remain a thing but the crosses, had the dome completely green, the walls of one side were pink and blacks, as the edges of a wound. One could not step on the ground without stepping on a spring.

They came next to the volcanoes; they passed by the antique cities: over there they were going; they did not stop. Lucia to the shade of her red sunshade, she felt like the mistress of that natural greatness, as if the whole world, where she made a great painting of it, was not been built for a thing but singing with its multiple tongues the loves of Lucia Jerez and her cousin. She saw herself the interior of her own cranium full of all those flowers: what happened always when she was alone, with Juan Jerez by her side. Adela and Pedro talked about quite formal happenings, those that had the virtue of putting Adela so contemplative and quite, giving Pedro reasons to go quite during the trip on the road, which he took advantage to celebrate with himself animated colloquia: every now and then there was some like: "Juan, how is Ana? I will stop for a minute, to see if Ana needs something". Lucia laughed, she was right, even when Sol was an honest girl, she had told her that Pedro Real looked very kind for her, she saw her having him on her soul: that did not look like a happy fact for Juan, although he hide it with prudence. Inside the car, joyful Sol was exclaiming: never, ever in her life of poor orphan, Sol had seen the rivers flowing, towards the forests strong little bells purple and blue, green and flourish in the fields. Out of a rose color of coral, her cheeks got colored, the onyx from Mexico never had such greater transparency than the fine skin of Sol, that morning of venture in nature. Ay! The good Ana smiled so much but she had forgotten to rise from her skirt the notebook.

* * * * *

Suddenly music played; the road darken itself, like a pleasant shadow, the mules slowed their speed, with a huge nose of buckles and bells. Into a jump Pedro was by the door of the car, right next to Sol, asking Ana what she needed. Here all of them went down, Sol turned soon to the car to be next to Ana and encourage her to take lunch as well as the others, seating on a rustic table, they were tasting with vehement appetite, relished by jokes by merciful Juan who was leading the table and attracting, so Ana would heard them from inside the car on her chair, brought to the purpose next to the table.

Over there, in the guiro cups on tripods of filaments that were just cut from the surroundings, milk was boiling, due the fragrant and foamy, just milked from the Durham cow that moved her pacific head for one of the clears of the twining plant. Since that place was such a pretty parador, with a green roof as a vinery all green, it was all set there by the owners of the farm so visitors would really have, once arriving from the city, their lunch in peasant style. Cheese, that would let milk dropping from it while cutting it, would taste so rich with the corn pies fuming, those served by the Indian girl dressed in a blue skirt, covered with white cloths. There were some hard eggs, whites, they were reclined, each one of them on a guiro cup, on herbs of pleasant flagrancy, they smelled like flowers. Over there, in the same shell of the coconut just cut in half, the milk of the fruit, with a little spoon of worked coconut that would take it off its natural cups. While lunch, Indians, barefoot on their canvas dresses, on the ground their palm hats, they touched, under another little further parador, right for them, some airs very soft with cord music, that softly template by the morning air and the thick twining plant, it was coming to our happy travelers as a charm. Adela just smiled as being forced to do it so. Violence was needed for Sol to not clap her hands in the car. Lucia frown very ugly once Juan got next to the car by Ana's side, he talked to her, making her smiling for a few minutes: When she heard Sol laughing, Lucia left her chair, so she went to the door as well. Ea! Ea! Diana is playing, is the playing for welcome and good-bye, the skillful Indians. The little Indian on the blue skirt gives the curious cow one of the abandon coconut cups left over. On the coach-box Pedro and Adela: Lucia, less content, to the imperial with Juan. The house of the farm, all white, of fleshy roof, it is seen at short distance. Ana is going so pale; and the mules, smelling the crib, almost fly up hill on the road, under the thick vault of almond trees that fill the avenue with its rounded leaves and its green fruits.

* * * * *

Much, much happiness. Lucia was also happy, although Juan was not there. Why Juan was not there: the fight of the Indians, although those were days for rest in tribunals like schools, it was an obligation for him to come back to the little village, if he did not want a asphodel gentleman of the place, who had great friends in the Government, would steal with a reason or another the land from the Indians, the energy of Juan had finally achieved a point to be recognized in the fight. Indians had left church with their music, the Sunday before, it was know that Juan would not wait for the train of the next day: when they bring Juan the mule, saw they had adorned it all with stars and palm flowers, the village was following him, many of them wanted to follow him up to the city. A very old gentlewoman, who was walking with her stick as a support, brought him a scapular of the Virgin, a handsome girl, with one son on her back and other one on her arms, came with her husband, who was a handsome young man, at the head of the mule, put the little Indian up high so he would shake hands with the "good gentleman"; many would come with honey jars covered with mat well tied, or other gifts, as if they able to give for so much the haunches of the cavalry horse, very showy of that party; another old man, the father of that place, my sir don Mariano, who had never drank of a liquor, although he worked the one of his own crops, came, supported on his two sons, who were almost like senators in the village, with the arms high since he could see Juan, as he had seen a light he had been waiting his whole life: "Hug him-he said-. Let me hug him! Sir, this entire village loves you like a son!". In a way that Juan, who was touched by those charms, left the farm, two days after he had arrived to it, he knew the Indians, besides his effort, would be at risk of loosing their temporary possession, in wait of the definite one, Juan had achieved the judge to agree on-the judge, who had received a gift from a gentleman on a fine horse the day before.

* * * * *

Much, much happiness. Lucia herself, whom during the two days Juan was over there gave him occasion of wonders with such great changes of disposition that could not explain, due of their greatness and less rational than those he already knew, she was now as some one ill who is coming back from an illness.

The house was all the visitors, since its owners were not there by then, those who were as members of the family of Juan Pedro, at nights he would go out hunting, it was rabbit hunting season, so abundant over there. Of those he brought in the sack he never talked about, because Ana should never forgive it to him, since there are simple souls in this world who do not find pleasure in killing, to the same entrance of the cave where he has his prater and his family, to the poor animals who had exit to discover, to switch cribs, a little corner in the forest rich in herbs.

Rabbits, being so smart, tend to fall in the hands of a hunter; because they don´t hear quite well the noise, they pretend to be dead, so the noise of the scape would not make them noticeable, they close their eyes, as if with this the hunter would close his, who pretends on his side he is not looking at them, with the shotgun on his back, just to avoid an alarm on the rabbit who knows it, is gone, looking in other directions, on the rabbit nest, until with a jump step on it and capture it alive: one time he got three, very kind one, of a smoke color, that was for Ana: another was white, to whom he found a way to tie a blue ribbon on its neck, that was a gift for Sol; he brought the other to Lucia, it looked like a captive king, of a gray very hard, of furious eyes that would never get closed, in such a way that in the next two days, it did not want to eat, lowered its ears that it had hold upright, it bite the little chain that fastened it, with it on its teeth laid dead.

* * * * *

Outing, there were just a few. Without Ana, who should go out for them? With her it was not right. Neither Sol would leave Ana of good will; nor Lucia would have leave to such pleasure when Juan was not with her. Adela, yes, had grabbed friendship with a huge Indian woman who had privileges in the farm, lived in other nearby, where Adela spent great part of the day, talking about customs of those people with the gentle Petrona Revolorio: "I hope the Ms. would not believe I´m talking to her just as part of my service, but I have gained love for her". She was a robust woman and of a very nice way of walking, although she did all these on a pair of feet so small that there was no way Petrona come see "her children" without being asked to show them, which she did it as one who does not want to, mainly when she was in front of child Pedro. Hands would move even with her feet, sometimes the girls would charm and hold her hands; she wear a stripped skirt, a transparent muslin shirtfront, laced on her shoulders and would let her pretty arms naked as well as her high throat. Was her face of light and gracious features, in such a way her mouth, half way open in the middle and contracted into two dimples on both sides, she was not at all bigger than her eyes. Her little nose, short an a bit rounded and twirled to the tip, it was a naughty one. She had a narrow forehead, from it to its back, in two bands not so smooth, the black hair, that in two copious braids, veined with a red ribbon, she had them contracted into a ring of hair, like a crown, on the high of her head. She always was wearing a stripped shawl down to one of her shoulders; everybody, when she said a phrase that sounded intentioned, would turn towards her back with more vigor the stripped shawl. Then she started running, smiling and talking into a jargon that presume to be so elegant and a citizen; she went to take care of Ms. Ana, which she did it so well, she prepared tamales of sweet coconut and a light chocolate, the thing she more pleasantly was drinking, due the cleaning and the freshness of it, that was something our dear ill girl had. While Ana enjoyed them, Petrona Revolorio, with her shawl crossing, was seating to her feet "not for a mere service, but because she had gained love for her" and told her stories.

There was no dawn without Petrona Revolorio being at the door of Ana's room with her basket of flowers, those she herself wanted to put into the glass and see them with her own eyes, how the girl was doing? "My little girl: look at her how elegant is looking today!; I'll tell it to sir Pedro so he will bring us a dance inviting the gentle women, we'll take her to dance with sir Pedro. He's such an elegant gentleman, sir Pedro! Look, my little girl: am not bringing to you the large and white Jessamine, since these from over here smell too strong; here I put this blue glass, these San Juan Jessamine, these flourish all year long over here and they smell so good at night. So, my little girl, get ready for the dance, I will let you use a shawl of incarnated silk I own, you'll look prettier than the same Miss Sol. I realize sir Pedro is dying for Miss Sol! I don't know what the little girl Adela has, she is like bored. Does my little girl want the coconut tamales today, or fresh meat? Yesterday I killed a pink sheep, which is so soft, meat is like a merengue! Jesus, my little girl, don't tell me that! I die for serving you: you see I am like the coconut little cups, that say in handsome letters: `I serve my mistress'. I'll prepare the door of house with flowerpots, and I'll rent musicians, the day my little girl come see me. I don't do that for anybody else: because I don't do it for a mere service, but I do it because I have gained love for you!".

    * * * * *

Pedro, with the absence of Juan had become the servant of the four girls, what else but keep supporting them, better yet when Adela was not around, even better when he was not close to Ana, who did not make good eyes when seeing Sol and Pedro, better than ever when by a chance Lucia and Sol were alone? Lucia had always chores, going very quite to see if Ana was sleeping, checking if they had watered the little blue birds, asking if they had brought the fresh milk that Ana should have right after waking up: Lucia always had, when Pedro and Sol could stay by themselves, something to do.

The place for conversations was a spacious shed, the pavement polished with little boards: the balustrade-as the rest of the house, was wooden-open in three sides for the three stairs that lead to the garden in front of the house. The shed was always under the shade, because an extremely copious twining plant covered it, embellished from space to space by clumps of little red flowers. They were hanging from the painted roof the fresh of capricious garlands with leaves and flowers as those of a twining bindweed, some wire pots covered with red wax, so they looked like corals, all them full of natural little flowers, shining and small, often adorned with filaments of a parasite plant that would grow on old trees at the farm, it was, due its white, light-green and growing into threadlike, looked like the gray hair of that grove. On the spaces on the wall, between the interior windows, embellishing with lines of dyed flesh color, there were such huge studios of flowers on wood, painted with their natural colors by the artists of the country, with great precision and style: two of the artworks were of Magnolias, one almost open, with certain beauty as an empress; the other one was still closed on its own branch: two more paintings were of pompous flowers from the Pacific Sea, with their leaves of intense red, clumped in a way that made them look better with their natural beauty and size.

There, under the soft shade, Pedro was telling European wonders and glories to Ana, who was hearing him with charm-to Adela, who acted as she did not care about them-,to Lucia, who thought with lovely anger about Juan, about Juan, who should not be coming back, because Sol was there, about Juan, who should come since Lucia was there-and he also told those stories to Sol, who listened them without emotion nor with displeasure and with her habits of an orphan girl, embarrassed sometimes for the sudden rudeness that tempered Lucia then with unexpected gestures of affection, she only felt the mistress of herself while she was next some one who needed her, not with Adela, who looked like avoiding her, nor with Lucia, although these hurt her so bad, she felt the same nature and abandon from Ana, from Ana to whom those warm and aromatic airs had given her back, not only the color of her face, but certain ability to move and some least of life.

Pedro found astonishment on the impudent and naughty way of extreme celebration where it is reduced, almost all the times paid back right away with usury by women, all the mysterious art of wooers, it was not possible for him such things with that girl who just had graduate from school, who with honest humbleness, looking at the eyes with no fear, said out loud as a matter of general conversation what Pedro left with more private purpose going discreetly to her ears. The girl had such a beauty that carried with herself, the majesty that defended her; it was becoming usual for her to go see whether the little blue birds had enough water, or if the fresh milk had arrived, not letting the conversation between Sol and Pedro, open for everything else and not very pleasant, about the issue where they were before Lucia went see the little birds. There was such an annoying thing for Lucia; finding them talking when she came back, about yesterday hunting, about the wild boar being prepared, about the celebrations after hunting in European castles, about the poor Ana, about the coconut tamales by Petrona Revolorio. Sol took Pedro, who was considered so scary by other women, with tranquility, whether when he read Amalia by Mármol or María by Jorge Isaacs, those novels that had been sent from the city, either to cover the table that the principal was embroidering, or, to hammer their brains.

* * * * *

-Yes, yes, she was so beautiful today. You tell me, mirror: Did Juan love her? Would Juan love her? Why am not like her? I will scratch my flesh: I will open my cheek with my fingernails. Imbecile face, why am not like her? Today she was so beautiful. Her blood was seen and her aroma could be smelled under her white muslin.

Lucia sitting, alone in her bedroom on a chair with no back, without getting undressed, even after midnight, a bit later she would stand up, she saw herself on the mirror again, and sit again, her face between her hands, her elbows on her knees. Then she started talking to herself:

-I see myself, yes I do. What is wrong with me that I see myself ugly? Am not, but am being it. Juan will notice it: Juan should notice am being ugly. Oh! Why am so afraid this way! Who is better than Juan in the whole world? How come he does not love me, if he loves every one who loves him? Who, who is the one who loves him the most, more than I do? I will lay by his feet. I will always kiss his hands. I will always hold his head on my heart. These cannot be even said, these things I would love to do! If I can do it, he would feel how much I love him, so he would not be able to love someone the way he´ll love me. Sol! Sol! Who is Sol to love him the way I love him? Juan!... Juan!...

While holding her voice she walked to the open window, she had her hands acting with no interest, calling Juan even when she had just wrote a letter without telling him to come back.

She pushed the two leaves of the window in a violent way, knee next to it, let her head out, as trying to get the air on it and make it wet on it; holding her head on the frame board, without bothering on having it on that wooden pillow.

-This cannot be! It can´t be!-getting up soon-: Juan will love her. I know him every time he sees her. He smiles with a charm that make me crazy. One can see on him, one can see that he feels pleasure to see her. Then that imbecile girl is too kind! It is not a lie, no: she is so kind. I, I don´t love her? Yes, I love her and I hate her! What I know, what is going on in my mind? Juan, Juan come here soon; Juan, Juan, don´t you come over here!

How come Juan should not love her?-the unhappy girl said, between hits of tears, a few moments later, being the crying of Lucia so strange, since it did not come abundant and then, alleviating the on crying, but on intervals, suffocating herself, exalting herself, similar to the water when falling down, between rocks, among the torrents-. How come Juan should not love her, since there is nobody who loves the beauty more than he does, is the Virgin of Mercy as beautiful as she is? Juan.... Juan...-she said in low voice, as for Juan would come without being noticed-; without Sol seeing him!

If he come ... what if he sees her... I, cannot stand it if he sees her! ... Not even if he look at her! If he is here one month, two months. What if she does not love Pedro Real, because she does not, and what if Ana tells her not to love him. Then she will love Juan, how come she will not love him? Who is the one who does not love him when she look at him? Ana would have love him, if she did not know he already loved me; because Ana is so kind! Adela loved like crazy; I noticed it so well, but he cannot love Adela. Why Sol should not love him? She is poor; he is rich. She will notice that Juan is looking at her. What a better spouse she can have but Juan? She will take him off from me, she'll do it if she want to. I have noticed she wants to steal it from me. I notice how she listens when he is talking; same way I listened to him when I was a little girl. I notice when he leaves, she rises her head just to keep looking at him. They will be here for one month, two months! She is always with Ana, everybody is with Ana all the time. He recreating the eyes in all his handsomeness. I, quite, by his side, with the lips full of horrors am not saying, hateful and furious. These cannot belong, it is impossible, impossible. Either Sol is gone, or I will go away. How come I should go away? So, one will steal him from me if she can!-she open her arms in the middle of the room, as challenging, the black hair felt unfasten on her back.

I hope they will not seat together: I hope I will not see that!

With her lips supported on her closed fist, she remained slept on a couch by the window, and her long black hair strangely shading her face with the air.

Who was the one Lucia saw the next morning, sitting on the shed, with Sol and Ana? Was coming with slow steps, as did not want to come.

Do not tell her, don´t you tell her!...-to Sol who was standing up just to warn her.

Lucia was coming with slow steps, Ana and Sol, who knew all the bedrooms in the house, they knew she was the one coming. Sol came back to her seat. Sol pretended he talked very animated with Ana and with her. Lucia came to the door. She saw them sitting together, they acted as they did not see her. She start shaking all. Get in? Get out? Juan! Over there Juan! This way Juan! She nailed her teeth on her lips and let them nailed on them. Turned her back, she entered the corridor that lead to her bedroom; said this to Sol who ran after her: "Go away! Go away!, and entered in her bedroom, closing and locking the door.

To Juan, who suppose she was embarrassed, he come back to the village of the Indians as fast as he could, from there, taking advantage of the light of the night to surprise Lucia with the light of the morning, he started restless his way back to the farm by horse in a hurry! To Juan, who had very deep loves in his soul, she consented him, for that mercy of his that was the greatest of her love, in holding his eagles to the hair of that creature, not so much for what he loved her, not meaning he would quit loving her, but for what she loved him! To Juan, put on the clouds of the sky and put on the sacrifices of earth her best charms, did not quit, however, for that excellent condition of his, of doing, thinking or omitting a thing toward he would believe he was pleasant to his cousin Lucia, although he did no the pleasure from her! To Juan, young man, as he was, he felt, in fact a forecast of a pain that seems more like a memory of his, as he was a very worked and elder man, to whom women, even more when they're young, looked like lovely ill ones! To Juan, who felt growing under his chest, in spite of his age, some like white beards so grown, as well as those pacific charms that are the only ones convenient for white beards! To Juan, the one who had virtue as ideas, so exalted gentle women, he understood they were as heinous as the gross guilt's the adulteries of the thoughts!

To Juan, because, after receiving those strange letters that Lucia had wrote for him at the farm without talking to him on his return to it, receiving him in such a way, with that way of looking, exploiting into that anger, with that disdain! When had stopped thinking Juan, when, thinking about that great charm he hold, without fatigue or falsehood, on his cousin, it was like a concession of his, like an acknowledgment of his, as a tentative, at the most, of grasping in body and seeing with the eyes of the flesh the ideas of a confused face and dress of pearls, that hold by the hands and with the wings open, they were flying in majestic turnings among the spaces of his mind? Since without the tender and fine soul he had supposed from his own will, as a natural essence of a body of a woman, in his cousin Lucia, what Lucia had become? Who is the man, who does not love a woman because of the spirit he supposes of her, or for the spirit he believe to see into her actions, for which she support and rise up his obstacles and ghosts in life? A woman with no tenderness, what is it but a glass full of flesh, even if it was made by Cellini, a glass full venom? In this way, in one day, men stop loving the woman who they wanted as crazy, when a clear and desperate action reveals them that in that soul there is no sweetness nor superiority they fantasized with.

-You think Lucia is ill. Ana-tell her I will salute her later-. Am going to see Pedro Real. Sol, thanks for being so good to Ana. You are already famous for your beauty, but I will give you fame of being so kind.

Lucia heard this, which made her temples blowing a buzzing sound and she felt she was falling on the ground: Lucia, who had open the door of her bedroom quietly and had come to the door of the living room, just to hear what they were talking about, walking on tiptoes.

* * * * *

They were so violent, ever since, the days at the farm. Neither Ana would know it, since she had Sol always by her side, what was the reason causing so much anger in Lucia. This anger stopped when Juan, taking her hand in the afternoon, took her, while Pedro and Adela were looking for sauce flowers for Ana, under the shade of a path of roses that lead to the sauce field, where there were from space to space some benches of stones, to the sides a music holder, of stones as well, like to put a book on. Both, in his look and his voice one could notice that Juan had something broken in his inside, some that was causing him sorrow; he was persuading Lucia with comforting voice, who reacted with futile excuses, so Juan did not conjecture right nor he would understand or excuse her, she was hiding the real reason of her anger, she wanted Juan to guess but not knowing at the same time: "because if it is not, and I told him, perhaps it will be! It is not, no, now I believe it is not; if he does not know what it is, who is he going to forgive me?". Upset with Juan in such an irrevocable way, as the clouds that pass on the sky were her funeral canvas, they got up as if they had found peace, but with no happiness.

The days turned so rainy, that neither Pedro went home, nor Adela to Revolorio's, nor Ana could go to the shed, nor Sol and Lucia, being anywhere else but close to her; nor Juan, beside his reading hours, that fatigued him now that he was not content, he had a way to be away from home. Fairly, there was not a greater pleasure for Juan, now that Lucia had showed her dried and arrogant spirit, not greater pleasure than being close to Ana, whom pure spirit with the short distance to death was getting clearer and finer. Juan was getting astonished, he was right, of passing that creature, yet free, by that creature who was exhaling herself, without dedicating his soul. This same contemplation of the spirit of Ana, whose capability of perfection and beauty then were absorbing her more than ever, they took her off risk, unavoidable in other occasion, by observing how they were united to Sol, without extraordinary flight of intellectual way, beauty and tenderness.

With Lucia, there were no peace. What did not penetrates Ana, how could Sol will understand it? In vane, Sol, although fearing already, taking advantage of the moments Ana was with Juan or Pedro and Adela, would go in search of Lucia, who found now ways to do long chores in her bedroom, where Sol entered one day almost by force, she saw Lucia in such a bad looking she thought it was not her, but other girl instead: a facing of a skirt on her waist, the eyes as burn and light, the face all as one who had cried.

That day Lucia and Juan were at peace: Juan did not allow, he believe that would be an indecency of his, that come and go of angers, that would take his soul off from him of fecund peace to which he had rights due the virtue of his excellence. That day, as Ana fatigued visibly of talking, Adela and Pedro were practicing on the piano a new song for Ana, Juan, a little bit upset with Lucia who show herself hard, talked to Sol for such a long time, so he felt animated about it, to see that the ill girl was hearing from the lips of Juan the story of Mignon, by the way of hers, the life of Goethe. This one was not for giving so much applause, from the part Juan was leading it by then, such beautiful things he kept telling, with that impetuous language of his, that would turn him on and would feel overflowing when he felt next to him pure souls, that Pedro and Adela, now a little bit more reconciled, they came discreetly to hear that new genre of music, a genre that was not criticized by the fraud of composition nor with pedantic pomp, but from the rich colors of nature was flowing with abundance from a naive spirit, in a way of oppressed confessions. Lucia was getting up, was showing very solicitous to Ana, she interrupted Juan in a very gentle way. She left acting with indignation. She entered passionate already. She sit, as she wanted to tame herself. "Sol, you think they watered the birds?". Sol went over there, and they had watered them. "Sol, have they brought the fresh milk for Ana?". Sol went over there, they had brought the fresh milk for Ana. Finally, Lucia exit, and did not come back: Sol found her later on, with the eyes dried and the waist licentious.

That was increasing. Today it was a hard time for Sol. Another one tomorrow. During the afternoon another one bigger. The girl, because Ana and Juan, did not say them. Juan was just coming down. Lucia, with great efforts, barely achieved, turned into apparent hate all the charm that she felt for Juan, pretending she did not and not making it perceptible. Who should blame on Sol so many moves, Sol whose pacific beauty in the country side got complete and her beauty was getting spread, since it was as she was pouring next to herself, for the spaces she walked they were, like her shadows, strength and energy? Sol, who risen her clean eyes over everybody else, huge and simple eyes, without stopping on one of them in particular; with Lucia, she always was tender; with Ana, a little sister; with Pedro, jovial and kind; with Juan, like thankful and respectful? That was her sin: her big, simple and clean eyes, which every time they were open, either for Juan, or somewhere else where Juan could see them, would penetrate as poison hooks by the jealous heart of Lucia; that beauty of hers, serene and decorous, the same beauty that always look with enchantment as the one of a clear night.

* * * * *

Until one night:

-No, Sol, no: stay here.

-Ana, where are you going? What's wrong, Ana? How can you leave this room at this time of the night? Ana! Ana!

-Let me go, girl, let me go. Today, I feel strong enough. Take me over there to the middle of the corridor.

-At the corridor?

-Yes: I'll go to Lucia's bedroom.

-Well, I'll take you there.

-No, my dear girl, no-she sit down for a moment, with Sol to her feet, she hugged her head, she kissed her on her forehead. She told her nothing, since she should not say a word to her. She got up, holding her arm.

-I know why Lucia is so sad. Let me go. Don´t you go for any reason. For the wellbeing of all. She went there, knocked on her door, and entered her room.

-Ana!

Ana, almost livid with her hands in such a way to balance and not falling on the ground, she was standing up, by the door of the dark room, dressed in white.

-Close, close the door.

It was talked so much, groans were heard, as from a chest going empty, they cried a lot.

By dawn, the door was open, Lucia wanted to go with Ana.

-No, no, I want to take you there; how come you´ll go alone when you cannot even remain on your feet? Sol must still be awake. I want to see Sol right now.

-You crazy! Until when you´ll be so kind, you crazy! For Juan, yes, when you see him tomorrow, which will be in front of me, kiss Jun his hand. For Sol, she should never know what was on your mind. Let´s go: take me to the middle of the corridor.

-My dear Ana, my little mom, my little mom!

Lucia cried that dawn, as much as one cries when he is joyful.

* * * * *

Part, party! The doctor have said it; the doctor who came from the city to see the ill girl, he found out Petrona Revolorio was right. Party of flowers for Ana!

All the musicians of the surrounding areas! Telegrams to the mocking birds! Messages for the yellow birds! Messengers all over the community, so the entire melodious and abundant sparrows will come! Ana, we all know about Ana: she is not doing well here, so she must go where she feels great! Petrona Revolorio had a great idea, the ill girl wants to give a dance so the farm would be famous. Petrona, of course, will not be at the living room, nor that will be the dance sir Pedro Real will host; she will be in a place where the her little girl Ana will see her, she will send all she need, because "she dance when she see every body else dancing, what she does is not for a mere service, but she does because she has gained affection for her". She is so content as she was the mistress. She has a China jar, on that existed who knows where, in what casts, she brought it, so it will adorn the party; she want it to be in place where the girl Ana will see it.

Now that the season of the farm has started! Go, well, go, Ana cannot; but Petrona is always with her and Sol, she, when Juan and Lucia go to the farm for an outing, then; what a coincidence! Then, Ana always needs Sol next to her.

The doctor came, after that night. Ana wants the dance to shake the spirits, to expel from the suspicious souls the heavy shame, so with the lonely touch the open wounds would not get any worse, so by looking at Lucia tender and affable, security in the soul of alarmed Juan would be recovered, so Lucia will look face to face with Sol in the time of triumph, as Ana will talk before to Juan, Lucia will not be shaking. Ana is gone, she knows it!: she does not want the dance for herself, but she wants it for others.

* * * * *

What a week, the week of the dance! Pedro has come to the city. For a moment Lucia wanted Juan to go instead, she changed her mind when she saw Ana!

-Oh, no, Juan! Please, don´t go.

There was a sadness mood on the eyes of Juan Jerez, nothing would make disappear that mood: sadness due the time when in the interior there is something broken, a dying believe, an absent vision, a fallen wing. In the eyes of Juan there was noticed a sweet look, not because he got happy of himself, but for the pleasure of seeing Lucia so sweet. Oh, how unfortunate are those with no sense of sweetness!

The best would come from the city; that´s why Pedro went there. Everybody wanted to make Ana feeling happy! Everyone wanted to see Sol del Valle who was more beautiful than ever, who would not? Horse cars and almost all the friends of the house. The road, except the space of the ancient city, was a valley. There were horse troops and cavalry. Near by the house, about two block away from it, they fixed for the cavalry two huge wooden houses, those were built years before for experiments of an industry that did not progress. Pedro, before leaving, had given instructions that all over the paths of the garden in front of the house, they put columns, like half a yard taller than a man, he said all of them must be decorated and cover by that parasite plant from the forest, planted here and there with blue flowers; on the capitals, some elegant pots will be set, dressed on filaments of twining plants and full of roses. The lights would come from a hidden place, in the garden, now in the house; Mr. Sherman was on her way, the all American owner of the electric light, so it would be very intense and abundant: the globes will be hidden between pots of roses. Jessamine, margaritas and lilies would dress Ana´s chair where she will sit on during the party, she will ever notice it. With a palm leave, set up on one side of the frameworks and curved in a gracious wavelike on the tip of the other one, they the Indians dressed all doors and windows, there was a way of adding the twining plants to the shed, other similar ones for a good space to both sides of the three entrances, in every steps, in every corner of the house, in the living rooms, they set up Japanese and Chinese glasses with American flowers. On the walls of the living room as a wonder out of use, Juan hanged four Castilian plates, those used by Spanish conquerors to inlay the towers. Inside and outside the white house, all over it but the shed, the floor was covered by a thick carpet of a golden black, which never reached black, with light and fantastic drawings, from which the one on the border was not less richer, rescuing the gravity and monotony that would have had without that mass of dark color.

* * * * *

People, cars, horses! Pedro and Juan were riding horses all afternoon long, from the house to the parador, and from it to the house. In the ancient cities where happy hostels still there and certain Indian who speaks French, almost all the guests have eaten. Dance starts at eight in the evening. It will last all night long. At dawn, breakfast will be at the parador. Oh, what a delicious tamales, from the most diverse species, Petrona Revolorio had prepared! This afternoon, when she made them, she wear the silk shawl. Ana has not seen her chair of flowers. Where Adela should be, but in the garden running, teaching all she knows, leading a bustle of flowers, flowers with black eyes?

What about Lucia? Lucia is at Ana´s room, she is dressing Sol. She will get dressed soon. Sol is first! Look at her, Ana, look at her. Am dying of jealousy. You see? The arm inlayed with laces. I take it; I kiss it for you! How great is loving someone! You tell me, Ana, here is her arm and here it is the pearl bracelet: which are the pearls? How Sol was dressed on? On muslin; of a white a little bit dark and transparent muslin, the chest barely open, letting one see her neck with no adorns around; the skirt almost hidden by the laces very fines that Ana had kept from her mother.

-What about the head? How you´ll comb your hair finally? I want comb it myself for you.

-No, Lucia, I don´t want to. You won´t have time. Now I´ll help you out. Am not going to comb my hair. Look; I will roll my hair up, in the same way I always have it, I´ll wear it as the day of the procession, and do you remember? I will wear a Camellia.

Lucia, acting like little crazy, pretended she was not listening to her. She messed her hair, she rolled up I a way she said: "This way? Right? I bit higher up, so it won´t cover your neck. Ah! What about the Camellias?... Those are the ones? How beautiful they are! How pretty!". The second time she said this slower and softer as she was lacking of strength and her soul was getting ruined about it.

-Do you really like them? What flowers you'll wear on?

Lucia, as confused:

-You know: I never wear flowers.

-Well: if you are not upset with me anymore, what did I do to make you angry? If you are not upset with me, wear the Camellias today.

-I, wearing Camellias?

-Yes, my Camellias. Look, here they are; I will take them myself to your room. You want me to do that?

Oh! If that entire beauty of Sol would be wearing your Camellias. Who, who will ever become as beautiful as Sol is? How beautiful, how beautiful these Camellias are! "What about you, what flowers you'll wear on?".

-I will..., look: Petrona brought these margaritas for me this morning, these margaritas.

* * * * *

People, cars, horses! Five, six, seven in the evening. The shed is full of people now.

Gentlemen and girls holding hands, from the interior rooms. Cars and horses stop by the back door, from where a carpeted corridor, with simple embroideries adorn the walls, leads to the interior rooms open from side to side and to the living room.

From it, when they get down off the car, they see at the entrance of the living room, where there are a double corner to set up two ottomans, as there were a forest of palms trees and flowers. In a room the gentle women let their coats and chattels and go to other room to fix and switch some of them their dresses that they had sent before hand. In other room the enter to get ready and to leave their arms, those who had come by horse. A panoply of Indian arms is nailed on one side of the door for gentlemen, that is a sign of their room. A big knot with colorful ribbons and a feather fan half open on the wall, reveal to the gentle women their stuff.

Graceful music is playing, that one played by the Indian of those surrounding lands, set up on the edges of the shed, they scratch the cords of their instruments. From the garden, the concurrents are coming; from the ladies room they exit; Ana holding hands with Juan. "Juan, who was it? Is it for me that chair of flowers?". Do not get too close to her; it is known you should not talk to her. Lucia is not coming? She will come right away. What about Sol? Where is Sol? They say she is coming. Young people get close to the door. She is not coming yet. Everybody is anxious. All dancing. Sol is finally coming: she is coming, without seeing her, she was calling at the room of Lucia. "Am coming! Here I am!". That is how Lucia responds from inside with a shaking voice. Sol does not hear the compliments they telling her: she does not see the living room that get curved to her steps; she does not know the sculpture did not give a better model than her head adorned with margaritas, she does not notice it, without being tall, all the rest of gentle women look smaller than her when close to her. She is walking as she is throwing clarities, towards Juan she is walking:

-Juan, Lucia does not want to open the door! I think something is wrong with her. The maid servant says she had gotten dressed three of four times, and she had undressed herself again, she had uncombed her hair, she had thrown herself on bed, desperate, hurting her face and crying. Then she sent the maidservant and she stayed getting dressed all alone. Juan! Go see what is wrong with her!

In this instant, there were Juan and Sol, in the middle of the living room and other couples, passing, waiting on the dance to get started, surrounding them.

-There she is coming! There she is coming!-Juan said, he was holding Sol by her arm, pointing to the back of the corridor, where in a faraway distance Lucia was finally coming. Lucia, all in black. At the time she was passing by the dressing room, interrupting the steps to an Indian, who was carefully taking outside, for the orders given by Juan, a basket full of arms, she saw, coming towards her holding hands, one next to each other, in full silver light, in the middle of the little forest of flowers that were at the entrance of the living room, she saw Juan and Sol, the most beautiful couple. She put her feet firmly as she was nailing herself into the floor. "Wait! Wait!", she told the Indian. She let Juan and Sol to get further in the narrow corridor, when she was about twelve steps away from them, from a terrible shaking from her head she unfastened her hair on her back: "Shut up, shut up!", she told the Indian, while pretending she was looking inside, she put her tremendous hand in the basket; when Sol was moving her hand away from Juan´s and was coming towards her with her hands open....

Fire! With a shot in the middle of her chest, Sol perplexed herself, feeling the air with her hands, like a dove palpitating and to the feet of Juan, she felt dead.

-Jesus! Jesus! Jesus! Twisting and scratching her dress, Lucia laid on the ground and dragged herself on her knees where Sol was, she messed her hair with her burn hands, kissed Juan on his feet; to Juan whose hand was being hold by Pedro Real so he would not fall. All the cares, all the cares for Sol! Even after she had died! All of them on her! Everyone wanting to give their lives to her! The corridor of gentle women crying! To her, no one would get close to her!

-Jesus, Jesus!-Lucia entered through the door of the dressing room for ladies, running away, until she got into a living room, where Ana was crossing half dead and Adela and Petrona Revolorio were holding her hands, exhaling a loud howl, she felt, feeling a kiss, in the arms of Ana.

ABOUT THE AUTHOR

Dear reader,

This is my translation for the first and only novel written by José Martí and published initially in "El Latinoamericano" a bimonthly newspaper in New York back in 1885. I want to take this opportunity to honor The Great Apostle of Our America.

In 1911 Gonzalo de Quesada writes an introduction for Amistad funesta. The novel was first published in "El Latino Americano" in 1885. This bimonthly newspaper was part of the Hecktograph Company based in New York. Gonzalo de Quesada also assures that there was no public library holding a sample of the novel. On its editions, this novel appeared to be written by the pseudonym of "Adelaida Ral". Therefore, the authorship of this novel was discovered by Gonzalo de Quesada when he found this newspaper with notes on it; notes by Martí. That was the office of the "Partido Revolucionario Cubano" (Cuban Revolutionary Party) as well as the office for Patria (Motherland) a newspaper that Martí administrated. The office of Patria was located on 120 Front Street in New York. One day while working in that office Gonzalo de Quesada found such artwork and asked Martí: "What is this, Master?" Martí answered in a kind way arguing that: "… memories of fights and sadness; but save them for another occasion. In this moment we should only focus on the magnum work; the only one worthy, the one of achieving independence".

I have been searching other translation/s into English of this novel, but still no news.

I think the English version of this novel will be favorable for those readers and critics who do not read in Spanish but are interested in the Latin American culture and literature. My intention is to promote more interest and studies to explore this branch in Martí´s literary work. His creative writing in this arena is not that abundant compared to his poetry and chronicle, however, one can find out important characteristics leading to the development of his narrative. Martí himself translated Called back by Hugh Conway and he gave it the title of Misterio (Mystery). Gonzalo de Quesada suggests that if Martí had more time for writing fiction he would have been quite successful in this field; he compares Misterio to the original of Ramona by Hellen Hunt Jackson, "ever found in libraries". These clues make me think of the achievements of Martí and his intentions to function as an interpreter to the Latin American readers; he also translated a lot into Spanish. From the novel Called back to articles such as "Brooklyn bridge" where he describes meticulously the details on the architectonic and design for the construction of the iconic bridge in New York.

Sincerely,

Juan Francisco Zeledón

Made in the USA
Columbia, SC
21 November 2020

25133884R00076